Landmark '

Wiltshire

Richard Sale

Published by
Landmark Publishing
Ashbourne Hall, Cokayne Ave, Ashbourne,
Derbyshire DE6 1EJ England

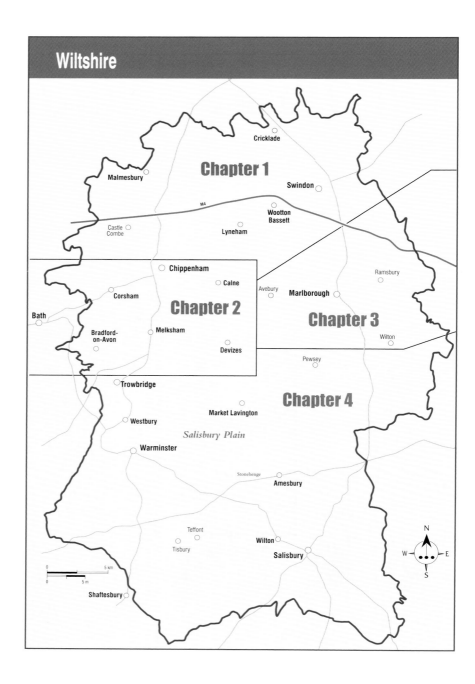

Avebury stones

Contents

Feature Boxes

No county in England, indeed no county in Great Britain, can compete with Wiltshire in its wealth of prehistoric sites. With both Avebury and Stonehenge, the two finest sites in the country, together with a number of other superb ancient and enigmatic places, Wiltshire is incomparable. It also has Salisbury, whose cathedral spire is the tallest in the country.

It has Salisbury Plain, an area of near pristine chalk downland, preserved by military occupation, and, in the Ridgeway, a road that many experts consider the oldest in the British Isles. It has more chalk carvings than any other county, including some famous white horses. It has canals from the great age of British waterways, and the headquarters of the Great Western Railway, which helped to bring about the end of the waterway age. In Savernake Forest, Wiltshire has one of the last large sections of original forest in southern England. Add fine towns and villages, once prosperous on the wool of sheep grazing the high downs, a collection of fine stately homes and excellent museums, and it is easy to see why Wiltshire folk – the Moonrakers

Top Tips

Avebury

Not as famous as Stonehenge, but with its associated Avenue, the site is just awesome. What was it that persuaded those long-gone people to create such a vast, stupendous and now so enigmatic an array of stones?

West Kennet Long Barrow

The best preserved Neolithic tomb in Britain. A magnificent construction and a great place to spend eternity, though now the human remains and artifacts have been removed, it houses only nesting swallows. From it there is a fine view of Silbury Hill, the most puzzling of all Wiltshire's ancient sites.

The Ridgeway

Neither mountainous nor craggy, in fact level and seemingly rather dull. But to walk in the footsteps of countless generations of ancestors while admiring views that stretch out seemingly for ever is a joy.

STEAM

Swindon is inexorably entwined with the history of British railways and this innovative museum is the ideal place to absorb it. Nearby, the designer outlet which now occupies Brunel's railway works will also appeal.

Malmesbury

Not just for the Abbey, but for the whole town which is a historical treasure house.

Stately Homes

With Longleat, Stourhead, Bowood, Wilton, Corsham and Lacock the visitor is spoilt for choice. It seems sad to have to choose just one, but if forced to do so it would have to be Lacock for its mix of architecture and the history of photography.

Salisbury Cathedral

Surely the most audacious building in the country. Come to admire the spire, but do not miss the cloisters and the best-preserved copy of Magna Carta in the country, or the fact that the cathedral stands in the most beautiful of closes.

Stonehenge

One of the most famous ancient sites in the world. How were the bluestones brought from Pembrokeshire? How were the trilithons erected? Was it really an astronomical observatory? Thoughtlessly hemmed in by roads it might be, but it is still superb.

Castle Combe

Arguably the most perfect small village in Britain.

Calne

A surprising choice perhaps, but the town has adjusted so well to the loss of its primary industry with new buildings and outdoor art works. Well worth the time to explore.

– believe their county is the most interesting in England.

Geology

Wiltshire is defined by chalk uplands, about two-thirds of the county lying on chalk, part of the broad band of chalk – known to geologists as the Southern England Chalk Formation – which links Dorset to the White Cliffs of Dover. To the north of the county the chalk is replaced by oolitic limestone, the characteristic rock of the Cotswolds. Indeed, a small section of the Cotswold Area of Outstanding Natural Beauty lies within Wiltshire. In a band from Malmesbury down to Bradford-on-Avon the houses are built of this 'Cotswold Stone', one of the most beautiful of all building materials. As Bradford-on-Avon is approached, the stone changes colour very slightly, becoming warmer. It is this stone from which the famous Georgian city of Bath is built, and Bath stone can also be seen at Bradford and the nearby villages. The addition to Bradford's name is from the river which cuts a valley between the limestone and the chalk. There are other valleys too, notably the Vale of Pewsey in the east of the county, and the Vale of Wardour in the southwest. In the south-eastern section of the county, close to the border with Hampshire, chalk is replaced by the sandy soils which underlie the New Forest.

A Brief History

The name 'Wiltshire' is said to derive from Wilton, close to Salisbury, which was the old county town. Wilton may itself be named from the River Wylye on which it stands. However, *wylt* is Old English for 'wild', suggesting to some that it may be the reason for the name, though why Wiltshire was any more wild than other English counties at the time is not at all obvious. Today's county is very rural, more so than many other counties, but in the days before industrialisation most counties were similar. Whatever the derivation of the name, it is clear that long before the word Wiltshire had passed the lips of an inhabitant, the county was an important place. It is not entirely clear why this might have been. Some have suggested that the existence of the forerunner of today's Ridgeway National Trail might have been an influence. It is often claimed that the Ridgeway is Europe's oldest road. That is, of course, debatable as there is limited hard evidence for its use before the coming of the Saxons. Palaeolithic (Old Stone Age) hand axes have been found near Marlborough, tempting some historians to claim that even before the last Ice Age – more than 12,000 years ago – folk were using the route. Though conjecture, this claim is not unreasonable: the Britain of that time, still attached to mainland Europe by a land bridge, was a dangerous place, the valleys filled with dense forest in which man was not only the hunter but the hunted – the less well-covered chalk ridge would have been a comparatively safe route. Neolithic (New Stone Age) and Bronze Age folk almost certainly used downland roads, their burial chambers being found close to it. Then, as now, people put their temples and cemeteries near the road.

Whatever the reason, it is obviously the case that the chalk downland of Wiltshire was an area of huge importance to prehistoric man. In Avebury and Stonehenge the county has the most important megalithic sites in Britain and, arguably, in Europe. There are also other sites from the same era which are almost as remarkable. Silbury Hill is the largest man-made site in Europe, in some senses a building project on a par with Egypt's pyramids. The West Kennett long barrow is arguably the most impressive Neolithic burial chamber in the country.

During the Iron Age the area maintained its importance, a string of fine hillforts being found across the county. The Romans utilised some of these, though Roman remains are actually somewhat sparse. There were settlements at Mildenhall (*Cunetio*), Old Sarum (*Sorviodunum*) and Sandy Lane (*Verlucio*), while the baths at Bath, just over the county border in Somerset, is one of the finest Roman sites in Britain. When the Romans departed the Romano-British re-occupied some of the hillforts, and if some experts are to be believed, the Ridgeway again became crucial to the history of Britain.

When the Saxons landed in eastern England they soon began their expansionist move west. At some stage they were stopped, a great battle being fought, and won, by King Arthur at Mons Badon. Whether there was a real man – probably a warlord rather than a king as we would understand the term – called Arthur is still hotly debated. But there seems little doubt that the British did indeed win battles against the Saxons. Nennius, a Welsh chronicler writing in about AD800, notes that Arthur won a series of twelve battles, halting the westward advance of the Saxons for a generation. The early battles in this series have been identified as being in the north of England, but the location of the greatest victory, Mons Badon, is disputed.

Many military historians have noted that a Saxon advance would have used rivers as the Saxons were undoubted masters of both the sea and inland waterways. The Saxons would therefore have used the Thames in their westward push, and also have used the ancient Ridgeway for a land-based advance. The British, descendants of the Iron Age (Celtic) hillfort builders, can be expected to have utilised the forts for defence. It seems possible therefore that the Downs were the scene of the battle of Badon. Badbury, close to Liddington, has been suggested as the origin of Badon, as has Baydon, a village to the east. Baydon lies on a Roman road and the remains of another fort lies close by. It has to be said, though, that Badbury Rings in Dorset (another hillfort) has also been suggested as a location for Badon, and there is no shortage of other suggestions. It is not, therefore, certain that Badon was in Wiltshire, but if it was, those who walk the Ridgeway may be walking in the footsteps of Arthur and his army.

But the Saxons were a patient enemy. After the defeats inflicted by Arthur they merely put down their swords and waited. Arthur seems to have been active in about AD500. By 565 the Saxons had been victorious at Barbury Castle: they had picked up their swords and moved west once more. In 577 at Dyrham, to the east of Bristol, they won a decisive battle, reaching the Severn and splitting the Britons in two (those in Wales, and those in the south-west, who were eventually pushed all the way to Cornwall). If the Saxon strategy had been to reach the Severn in order to split the Britons the Ridgeway would definitely have been the way to come.

Saxon England was a peaceful place, unless you happened to be living on the border between the great kingdoms of Wessex, Mercia and Northumbria. Wiltshire lay exactly on the Wessex–Mercia border, and saw years of conflict as kings battled for supremacy. Significant battles wee fought at Bradford-on-Avon and Great Bedwyn in the late 7th century. Peace was restored in the 8th century, but it was short-lived as Norse invaders attacked England, taking control of all except Wessex, where King Alfred put up fierce resistance. At first he was defeated and pushed back into deepest Somerset. But he gathered strength and eventually defeated the Norsemen at a decisive battle at Edington. Alfred also established towns in the north of the county as a bulwark against further Norse invasions.

Ultimately the Norse were successful in taking Wessex, a decisive battle being fought at Sherston, and England was ruled by Norse kings, though the Saxons had regained the crown shortly before the Norman Conquest. The Normans brought stability, many of the county's churches being built or begun in their early years.

Wiltshire was, in the main, for Parliament during the Civil War. Many county towns have stories of local skirmishes, but ironically the only major battle fought in Wiltshire, at Roundway Down, was a decisive victory for the Royalists. After the battle they captured Bristol, then besieged Gloucester and appeared on the threshold of overall success. The tide turned against the King, but the battles which were to ensure his downfall were fought away from Wiltshire.

With peace restored, the downland which had been so important to early settlers proved to be so again. Sheep

The Moonrakers

The story goes that a hundred years or more ago, local smugglers, having hidden kegs of contraband brandy in a village pond, were using hay rakes to retrieve them one night when the excisemen arrived. When asked what they were doing, the smugglers claimed they were trying to retrieve the cheese they could see in the middle of the pond. Realising the 'cheese' was the full moon's reflection, the excisemen laughed their way out of the village and spread the word of the Wiltshire 'Moonrakers'. The story of these idiot county folk spread and soon Moonraker became a general name for anyone from Wiltshire. Though meant to be demeaning, Wiltshire people know that the name is far from being so, suggesting instead a resourcefulness which is admirable.

The location of the actual pond which gave birth to the Moonraker story is disputed, but expert opinion favours Crammer Pond at the eastern end of Devizes, where a plaque to the original Moonrakers has been erected.

Above: Bowood House
Below: Stonehenge

reared on the downs provided the wool that was to be the mainstay of the county's economy for over a century, just as the high land of the Cotswolds, to the north, was to be for that area. Many of the county towns owed their prosperity to the wool trade, its wealth raising the buildings that are such a feature of both the towns and the county in general. In the early 19th century canals were built, which aided county prosperity, and when railways supplanted canals, the county was at the forefront of the revolution again, Isambard Kingdom Brunel choosing Swindon as the headquarters of his Great Western Railway. The Swindon site is still a place of pilgrimage for those fascinated by the steam age.

But despite the industrialisation which the railways brought and supported, Wiltshire remains a county where the landscape is rural rather than urban, though modern amenities are not lacking. A county well worth visiting.

Food and Drink

Among food lovers Wiltshire is as famous for its hams as it is for Stonehenge and the spire of Salisbury Cathedral. Pig breeding and Wiltshire have gone together since Saxon times, when Alfred the Great created his settlement at Cricklade, ensuring that incomers were given sufficient land with their properties that they could grow their own vegetables and keep a pig. From then until times beyond the Industrial Revolution dwellers in this most rural of counties have kept pigs – this may well be the origin of Swindon's name: *Swine down* – and enjoyed a menu in which pig meat, in various forms, played an important part. The body meat of the pig was used for roasting joints and making bacon, but the legs were for ham, and there were two methods of manufacture, both of which can still be found within the county. The traditional Wiltshire ham is dry cured with a covering of bacon and molasses. More exotic is Bradenham ham, named for the last Lord Bradenham, who reputedly invented the process in the late 18th century. The ham was first marinaded in molasses, coriander and juniper, with a pinch of other spices, for about two weeks, then hung to mature for anything from three to six months. The result was the formation of a distinctive black rind, and an equally distinctive flavour.

Although ham production has been maintained in the county, some of the other recipe ideas for sections of the pig have died out over time as people have become more affluent. Trotters were boiled long enough to allow them to be eaten, usually when cold; small intestines were turned inside out, boiled and eaten, hot or cold, as chitterlings; heads were boiled, the meat carved off and placed in jelly formed from the liquor to be eaten as brawn. Today few people find these dishes very palatable, though some other ideas still have a dedicated, if small and perhaps dwindling, clientele. Pig blood is made into black pudding, while faggots are made by chopping up various offal, including liver and lights (i.e. lungs), mixing with onions, various herbs and breadcrumbs, then rolling into small balls held together with a mesh of caul, the lace-like membrane which surrounds the pig's stomach and

The Downland Drove Road

The Ridgeway, the path on the high downland, was used through medieval times, the route eventually becoming a drove road. In the days before refrigeration animals were brought to town on the hoof, for slaughter and immediate sale. The herds were controlled by men employed specifically for the task, drovers who used ancient tracks to avoid the rutted muddy trails that most roads of the time were, and to stay close to free fodder for the herds. A drove would have been a fine sight for not only were cattle, sheep and pigs herded, but chickens, geese and turkeys too. The poultry had their feet encased in pitch to withstand the rigours of the journey, and bulls were shod to save their hooves from cracking under their weight; it is said (and easily believed) that the men who shod the bulls were both brave and skilled, and earned every penny of their fee. Before reaching the downs, the droves passed through the towns and villages of west Wiltshire, adding their animals to the county's thriving meat producers.

digestive organs. Just reading the recipe makes the author somewhat queasy, but his father swore that there was no better dish in the world than baked faggots with peas.

Bacon was another county favourite, with various methods of curing developing, including smoking with different woods. Bacon fraise was the meal of choice for medieval agricultural workers. It was made by frying bacon, then covering it with an egg batter and baking. One slab could keep a hardworking man going all day.

The liquor from boiled pig sections was the basis of the jelly which held the ingredients together for the pork pie, another speciality. Devizes has its own pie, this one having veal, lamb and vegetables added. Sausages were also made from meat scraps and various filers. At Trowbridge the firm of Bowyers, started by Abraham Bowyer in the early 19th century to make bacon, sausages and other pork-based products, became a county institution, as well as a major employer, and the decision to close the factory and move production to Nottingham in April 2008 was a major blow to both the employees and tradition.

The liquor from boiled pig products was also the basis of the other county speciality, lardy cake, a very rich mix of lard, bread dough, sugar and dried fruit.

No other local dishes can really compare with what can be achieved starting with a pig – it was famously said that the only thing Wiltshire people did not eat was the squeal – but there are some interesting cheeses. North Wiltshire Cheese was mentioned by Jane Austen, but eventually saw its popularity dwindle in the face of the Cheddar from nearby Somerset. Today it is being made again; a firm, tangy cheese.

There are no county drink specialities, but local beers and ciders do have strong supporters. Visitors wishing to try these, and local food produce, should head for the North Wiltshire Food and Drink Festival, usually held in early September at various locations. Both Marlborough and Salisbury also have food festivals during the summer.

Wiltshire

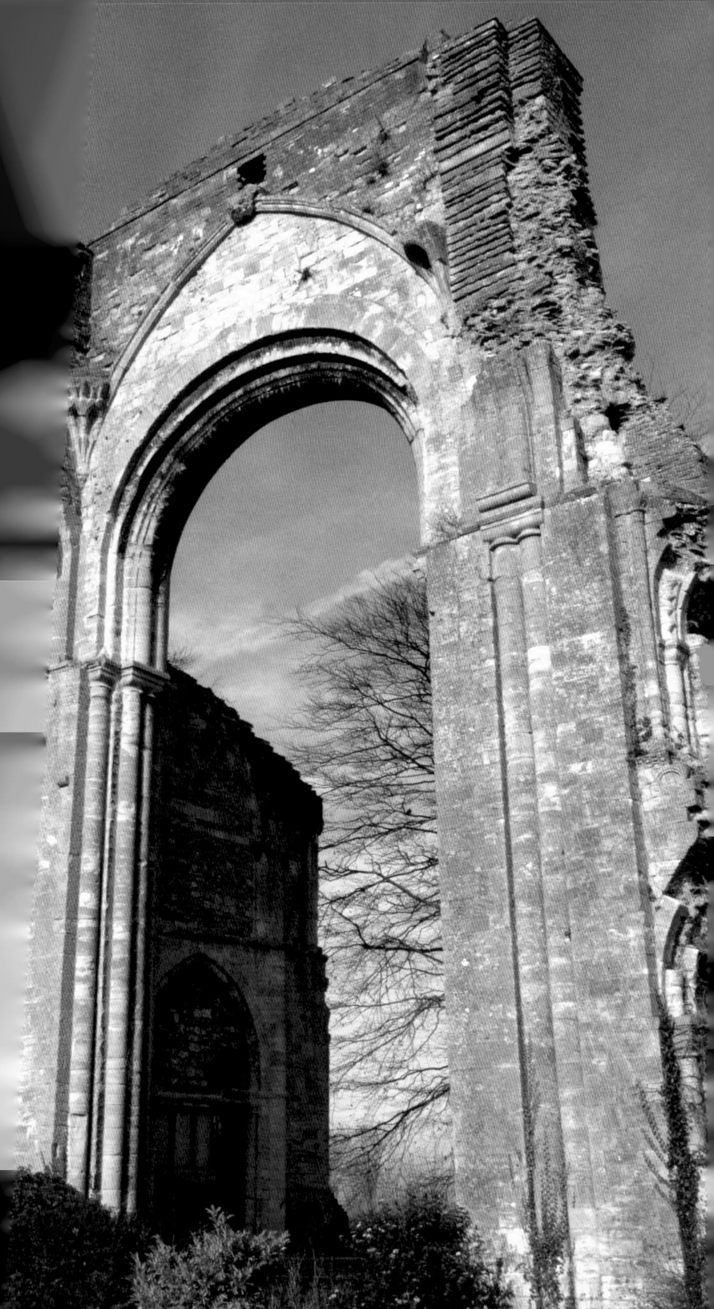

In this first chapter we head north, exploring towns created by King Alfred as a defence against rampaging Norsemen, taking in a fine old abbey and one of the prettiest villages in England, as well as visiting the county's largest and most modern town, one which played a significant part in the history of British railways.

To the north, Wiltshire pokes stubby fingers of land into the Cotswolds. **Cirencester**, a town with enviable Roman remains and a fine Cotswold church, is just a few miles on the Gloucestershire side of the county border, as is the equally well-known Cotswold town of **Fairford** (today rather more famous perhaps for its air base than the stained glass in the church). Even closer to the border are **Down Ampney**, famous as the birthplace of Ralph Vaughan Williams, and **South Cerney**, close to which – and over the border in Wiltshire – the flooding of old gravel pits and land reclamation have created the **Cotswold Water Park**, which offers most water-based sports, and **Keynes Country Park**, which has a golf course and waterside barbecue area. Lakes 46 and 48 of the Water Park, reached from a car park on the road which links Somerford Keynes with Minety, form the **Swillbrook Lakes Nature Reserve**, which is excellent for wildfowl and reed-loving birds, as well as its plant life. Unusual species to be found here include the nightingale and the southern Marsh-orchid, while at least 13 species of dragon- and damselflies breed.

Cricklade

The Water and Country Parks are easily reached from the A419. This (relatively) recent dual carriageway was engineered to allow easy access between the M5 at Gloucester and the M4 at Swindon and follows the line of the Roman **Ermin Way**. Travelling south along it the visitor passes the slip road for the Water Park to reach one for **Cricklade**, the first town on the River Thames. It is thought that there may have been a settlement in Roman times as the Thames was navigable from London to here, suggesting a port close to Ermin Way. The present town dates from the time of Alfred the Great, who needed a fortress town to aid the defence of Wessex from Norse invaders. Cricklade has been called 'the most intact Saxon new town in Britain', though it is the layout rather than the buildings which indicate its history. Owners of properties on the High

Highwayman Hanged

No. 58 High Street, to the left as visitors explore, was once the home of William Peare, a 24-year-old man who drank regularly in what was then the Three Horseshoes Inn opposite. Peare robbed several stagecoaches during a short career as a highwayman. Eventually, in 1783, his luck ran out. He hid out in the roof space of his house, but the house was, of course, the first place that was searched when officers who had discovered his name came looking for him. He was caught as he attempted to escape and was subsequently hanged. As was the custom at the time, Peare's body was left to rot on the gibbet as a warning to others tempted to follow his criminal ways, but one day it disappeared. It is thought that friends had taken the body one night for a secret burial.

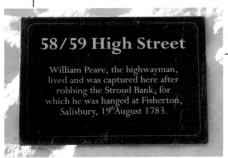

Highway Plaque, Cricklade

Street in Saxon times were allocated a plot of land 2 poles (16½ft or 5m) wide and 12 poles (198ft, about 60m) deep. The frontages of the shops and houses on today's High Street still maintain the 2 poles width.

The size of the building plots was generous, an encouragement to settlers, but in exchange those who came had to agree to fight to defend the town if the Norsemen came. So important was Cricklade to the defence of Wessex that it was granted a mint, silver coin being produced here. Later the town profited from a reduction in taxes granted in a charter of Henry II. The King was expressing his gratitude to Cricklade for having shown kindness to his mother Matilda, when she was fleeing King Stephen during the Civil War of 1135–54. Cricklade is also one of the few towns in England which maintains the offices of a Court Leet. The Leet was set up in medieval times to oversee all aspects of the town's affairs, rather in the way in which the Town Council does today. The Leet was presided over by the Lord of the Manor and included such officials as the Hayward, who looked after grazing rights, and the Ale Taster, who ensured local inns were not short-changing their customers by selling watered-down or otherwise inferior beer. The Taster is still an officer of the Leet, as visitors can verify by asking to see the certificate declaring that ale served is 'wholesome and fit for the people of Cricklade' at any of the local hostelries. At one time the Ale Taster would have worked hard – there were once 22 inns and pubs in the town. That number may explain the fact that the town also had a large number of churches for its population. Today one of four leaflets which help visitors follow circular walks around the town and the immediate locality is entitled 'The Nine Churches Walk'.

Those approaching Cricklade from the A419 pass the **Town Museum** (to the right), with its collection illustrating town history, to arrive at a T-junction opposite the impressive **Jubilee Clock**, erected in 1898 to commemorate Queen Victoria's Diamond Jubilee. A right turn here follows High Street northwards. No. 14, to the left, is a 16th-century timber-framed hall.

Beyond the plaque to Cricklade's infamous robber, William Peare (see feature box), and also to the left is **St Mary's Church**, probably the town's first church, positioned just inside the Saxon north ramparts. It was rebuilt by the Normans, but declared redundant in the 1980s. It was then taken over as a Catholic church, one of only a few in the county. The building, with dormer windows beneath a Cotswold slate roof, looks almost as much domestic as ecclesiastical and is a delight. Inside the surviving Norman chancel arch is excellent, as is the 14th-century cross in the churchyard. Continuing north, though it a fair step and many will choose to drive, the visitor passes through the old Saxon ramparts, still just visible to the left, close to the river, crosses the Thames and continues to reach the **North Meadow National Nature Reserve**. The reserve is a traditional hay meadow and is the premier site in the country for the snakeshead fritillary, a very beautiful member of the lily family.

If, instead of turning right along High Street a left turn is taken, the visitor soon reaches a right turn into Church Lane. Follow this to reach **St Sampson's Church**, by the yard of which stands the old **Market Cross**.

Although St Mary's is probably older, there has been a church here since the late 9th century. The dedication is curious, Sampson was a Welsh saint, a somewhat curious choice for a Saxon town. Though Saxon in origin, the present church is Norman, built in the 13th century. The imposing tower was added over an 80-year period ending in 1558. The school later became the town's workhouse. It is now the parish hall. Back on the High Street, continue south to see No. 23, to the right, a very fine Queen Anne house.

Those interested in churches want to head west from Cricklade to **Leigh**, where the chancel of the old church can be seen in a field close to the source of an early tributary of the Thames (one claimed by some, but with little support, as the true source of the river). The bulk of the church was removed to a drier location in the 1890s, leaving just the chancel with its superb early medieval features − arches and windows − and extremely unusual 17th-century texts on the walls. An alternative, but equally unusual church lies to the south of Cricklade, at **Purton**. **St Mary the Virgin** has a tower at one end and a spire at the other, one of only three parish churches in England with this combination. Inside there are excellent 14th-century wall paintings. The village also has a museum of local items and a vast tithe barn. Purton is reached by heading south along the B4553 from Cricklade, the road passing close to the southern ramparts of the Saxon town. Purton is actually a turn right off the B4553, the main road soon reaching the **Swindon and Cricklade Railway**. The railway, once part of the Midland

and South-Western Railway, originally linked Cheltenham and Andover. It was completed in 1891, but closed to passengers in 1961. A volunteer preservation society was formed in 1978. The line is now open from Blunsdon Station, near Purton to Hayes Knoll, but the intention is to add further track in the future. The railway has a museum with historic carriages and wagons, and other memorabilia. Trains also run at weekends, occasionally drawn by steam engines.

From Purton it is just a short road journey to Swindon, while for visitors who enjoy Cricklade, then a return on the A419 to Swindon is a fast trip along the dual carriageway, passing the massive Honda car factory.

Swindon

Swindon is Wiltshire's biggest town. With a population of about 160,000 it is about three times the size of Salisbury and almost five times the size of Trowbridge, the county's capital. In the Domesday book the town is *Suindune*, probably from *swine dun*, pig hill, though some experts believe it could be from *Sweyn's hill*, Sweyn being a relatively common Saxon name. The Saxon settlement was on the hill which guarded the entrance to the Vale of White Horse to the east, but they had been preceded by several centuries by the Romans; a villa haa been excavated at Groundwell Ridge at the northern edge of the present town.

By the medieval period this hill-top settlement had grown into the most important local market town. The oldest area of the town – called **Old Town** as one might expect – is a de-

lightful area of quiet alleys with some of the best restaurants Swindon has to offer. Here too are the **Old Town Gardens**, laid out in Victorian times and retaining the sense of unhurried decorum that was intended. Such a fine example of their type are the gardens considered to be that English Heritage have judged them a Grade II site on their register of the country's parks and gardens. The gardens are home to the annual MELA festival of Asian art and culture. Also in Old Town are the **Arts Centre**, which hosts a programme of music (of all forms), comedy, drama and film throughout the year, as well as regular exhibitions. Swindon also has a second theatre, the **Wyvern**, closer to the town centre.

At the western edge of the Old Town is Swindon **Museum and Art Gallery**. The museum has an interesting collection on local history, including items from the Groundwell Roman villa, but also items on local geology and some from much further afield, such as an Egyptian mummy of a young boy and a stuffed Indian crocodile. The art gallery has a collection of contemporary British work.

Industrialisation brought prosperity to Swindon, Isambard Kingdom Brunel choosing it as the site of the railway works for his **Great Western Railway** in 1840. A local legend has it that Brunel was surveying the line of his railway from London to Bristol and had stopped for lunch close to Swindon's Old Town. His assistant asked him where he intended to build the works for the railway and Brunel tossed the remains of his sandwich in the air and declared it would be where the crust

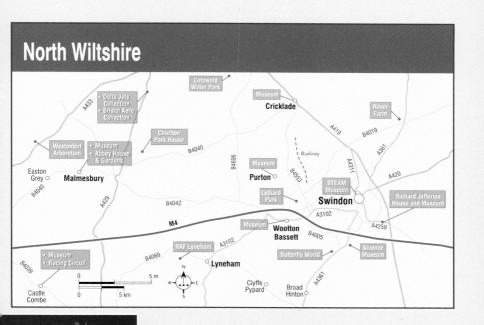

North Wiltshire

Cotswold Water Park

Museum
Cricklade

Rover Farm

Delta Jets Collection
Bristol Aero Collection

A433

Charlton Park House

A419

B4019

A361

Westonbirt Arboretum

Museum
Abbey House & Gardens

B4040

B4696

Railway

A4311

A420

Museum
Purton

B4553

STEAM Museum

Easton Grey

Malmesbury

A429

B4040

B4042

Lydiard Park

Swindon

Richard Jefferies House and Museum

A3102

A4259

M4

A3102

Museum
Wootton Bassett

B4005

Science Museum

RAF Lyneham

B4069

Butterfly World

A361

Museum
Racing Circuit

Lyneham

B4039

Clyffe Pypard

Broad Hinton

Castle Combe

0   5 m
0   5 km

N W E S

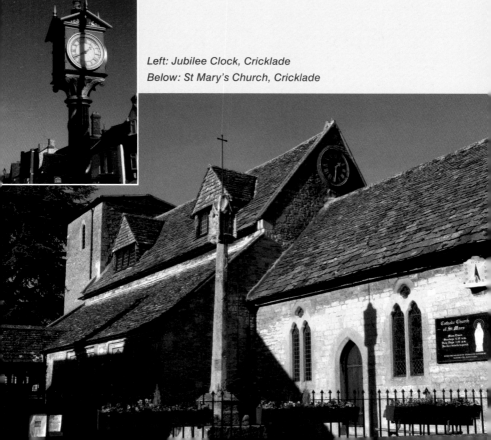

Left: Jubilee Clock, Cricklade
Below: St Mary's Church, Cricklade

landed. The story does not have quite the appeal of Robin Hood shooting his last arrow to decide his burial place, but does accord well with Brunel's flamboyance. Whatever the reason for the choice, Swindon became the heart of the GWR, the steam locomotives that for many still define all that is truly great about the railway system being constructed and maintained here. To house the railway workers a new town was constructed north-west of Old Town. The terraces of stone-built houses survive and suggest an enlightened attitude to worker welfare for the period. **St Mark's Church**, close to the railway village, was built with a combination of company money and subscriptions from the workers.

For many years the Old and New Swindon towns were separate entities, only amalgamating in 1900. For much of the 20th century the railway sustained the town, but after the 1939–45 war things altered. The age of the railway was replaced by the age of the car. The railway works declined, and Swindon with it. There was a significant revival in the latter half of the century with much talk of Swindon becoming the centre of the UK's answer to California's Silicon Valley, the 'M4 Corridor' bringing the world of new technology to Britain. Swindon Town football club won the League Cup and Anglo-Italian Cup, and promotion to the old First Division, and the town's fortunes seemed set to rise in similar fashion.

The true bonanza did not materialise. The football team were relegated to the League's basement division. The town fared better, becoming a thriving town with good leisure facilities (see the further information section at the end of the book) and excellent shopping centres. The old railway works have been transformed into **STEAM**, a superb museum of the GWR, one of the best museums in the county. Adjacent to it, the remaining works buildings are now occupied by the **Great Western Designer Outlet**, where famous fashion, accessory and sports names have shops, supported by cafes and restaurants. Also on the site are the Central Office of the **National Trust**, in a modern building which includes a shop and cafe, and **NMRC** (the National Monuments Records Centre). The Centre, housed in another former GWR building, has over ten million records, photographs, etc, relating to the archaeology and architecture of every town and village in England. The Centre has public search rooms.

The rebuilt town centre is also worth visiting for its shops, cafes and restaurants. Grouped around **Brunel Plaza**, with the great man's statue gazing out, probably in frustration at the limited imagination of modern building enterprise in comparison to his own efforts. East of it, on the campus of Bath University in Swindon, the **Museum of Computing** is a reminder of the promise of the M4 Corridor. Here exhibits chart the history of computers, calculators and computer games, with plenty of hands-on opportunities. Admission is free. One other site which is unlikely to be missed by those who visit by car is the **Magic Roundabout**. Any visit to the old GWR site or the town centre requires the negotiation of an interminable series of roundabouts, but the 'Magic', named after the children's' television favourite with which it shares no discernible characteristics, is a series of mini-roundabouts grouped around a larger one. The theory is that the design reduces confusion and speeds the traffic. In practice it often seems to reverse that concept.

Swindon can be used as a centre for several other worthwhile sites. To the south, at **Wroughton**, **Butterfly World** allows visitors to walk freely among hundreds of the world's most beautiful butterflies and moths. A recent arrival is the Malagasy Lunar Moth, which has an 8-inch (20cm) wingspan and a 6-inch (15cm) tail. There are also equally spectacular insects. The site has a cafe with a view of the butterflies, garden and aquatic centres and a craft village. The large hangars on the old airfield at Wroughton are an out-station of the **Science Museum** (whose main building is in London). At Wroughton larger items – aircraft, road transport, agricultural machinery and fire-fighting equipment – are stored. There are regular open days when the collection can be visited.

Close to Wroughton, at **Coate**, the house in which Richard Jefferies was born is now a museum to his life and work. Jefferies (1848–87) is considered one of England's most important writers on natural history, rural life and agriculture in late Victorian England. **Coate Water**, a reservoir in which Jefferies swam as a young boy, is now the centrepiece of a country park with a children's play area, pitch and putt golf course, opportunities for fishing and a nature reserve.

West of Swindon, **Lydiard Park** is the ancestral home of the St John family,

one of whom was created Viscount Bolingbroke by Queen Anne. The house was remodelled in Palladian style in the 1740s and has an exquisitely decorated interior with an abundance of stucco, wood and stone, as well as quality furnishings and good artworks. The house owes its present state to Swindon Corporation, which acquired it in when ruinous in 1943 and has restored it. The lower floor is open to the public. A one-time resident was Lady Diana Spencer, the second Viscountess Bolingbroke, who lived here in the late 18th century. The Viscountess shares an ancestry and a remarkable likeness with her more famous namesake. Outside the house the walled garden is a delight, as is the surrounding parkland. The little church of **St Mary** is considered one of the best small churches in England and has a marvellous life-size effigy of Edward St John in full battle dress: Edward was killed during the Civil War.

Finally, to the north of the town is **Highworth**, which John Betjeman described as 'one of the most charming and unassuming country towns in the West of England'. At the time of the Civil War the town, then more prosperous and important than Swindon, was loyal to the King and was besieged by Sir Thomas Fairfax after his victory at Naseby. The town was bombarded, the townsfolk retreating to the fortified church. Fairfax was, inevitably, victorious, many local people being killed. There are several fine buildings in the town, and nearby **Roves Farm** (at Sevenhampton, to the south-east) has much to entertain younger children, with a willow maze, electric tractors, pets corner, big bale stack and soft play area.

Above: The designer outlet in the old railway works, Swindon

Left: Mural of original railway works at the designer outlet

Below: Snowdrops at Lydiard Park

Bradenstoke Priory
and William Randolph Hearst

The village of Bradenstoke was the site of an Augustinian Priory founded in 1142. Today little remains visible. There were more substantial remains, particularly of the great tithe barn and Priory guest house, but in the 1930s these were purchased by the newspaper magnate William Randolph Hearst, who had them transported off-site. Some were moved to St Donat's Castle in south Wales, but the tithe barn was shipped to Hearst's 'castle' at San Simeon in California. It is believed that the barn was dismantled stone by stone, each stone being numbered to allow accurate re-erection, but by the time the crates had arrived Hearst had lost interest in the project and the crates were never unpacked. He later sold the crates to a local hotelier, who planned to use the barn for wedding receptions and other large-scale events. Permission to erect the barn was refused, as the proposed site was in the Californian earthquake zone and there were fears that the building, which could never pass seismic regulations, would collapse on the guests in the event of a quake. The crates therefore remain unopened. Recently some Bradenstoke residents have been attempting to get Lottery funding to buy the barn, to have it shipped back to Wiltshire and re-erected on site.

The nearby Clack Mount, close to the village, was probably a Bronze Age round barrow, later pressed into service as the base of a windmill.

West of Swindon

Heading west from Swindon on the A3102, the visitor crosses the M4 motorway and soon reaches **Wootton Bassett**. The town is first mentioned when it was granted to Malmesbury Abbey in the 7th century. The original settlement was in the valley; after that was attacked and destroyed by Norse raiders in the 11th century, the survivors moved to the top of the adjacent hill. The town's fortunes then grew and it became an important market town – indeed, of considerably more importance than Swindon. It is now a quiet, small provincial town with a High Street which echoes that of Marl-borough in being wide and straight. The buildings have less character, though there are some fine Georgian buildings. The **Town Hall**, dating from 1700, with its half-timbered upper storey supported by 15 stone pillars, can, however, hardly be said to lack character. It was built in the late 17th century by Edward Hyde, the town's MP. Hyde had an illustrious career, being an advisor to Charles I and going into exile with his son. Later Hyde became Chancellor of the Exchequer and Lord Chancellor and was created Earl of Clarendon in 1661. Later town MPs had much less creditable careers, Wootton Bassett being renowned as a Rotten Borough. The two MPs which the town sent to Parliament were elected by a public show of hands, with bribes being common and barely concealed. Indeed, the election accounts of one MP actually include the figure used to buy votes, either directly with monetary gifts, or by the provision of free beer. The Town Hall now houses the **Town Museum**, with a collection of photographs illustrating local life in the 19th and 20th centuries, together with some altogether more sombre items – the ducking stool, whipping post and stocks which were used to punish offenders in the 17th century.

South of Wootton Bassett are a collection of interesting villages, the best of which is **Clyffe Pypard**, where **St Peter's Church** is one of the most charmingly positioned in the county. The village is named for its position, set into a steep section of downland as it falls towards the Wiltshire plain, and for a 13th-century lord, Richard Pipard. With its backing of beach-shrouded cliff the village is wonderfully picturesque. The church dates from the 15th century, but has been drastically restored. Inside look for the pulpit, dated 1629 and beautifully decorated. The nave has an excellent wagon roof and there is a superb, life-size white marble memorial effigy of Thomas Spackman, a carpenter who died in 1786, leaving money in his will for the education of the village's poor children. Sir Nikolaus Pevsner, author of the *Buildings of Britain* series of books on county architecture, and his wife are buried in the churchyard.

Close to Clyffe Pypard are the sites of three medieval villages, built on the spring line of the chalk escarpment.

It is likely that they were not resettled after the Black Death had killed their inhabitants. Also abandoned was the Norman motte and bailey castle of **Bincknall**, built on a chalk spur overlooking Wootton Bassett. There is little to see, but it can be reached by a footpath from **Broad Hinton**, another picturesque village lying just off the main road. The church is worth visiting for the number and quality of its monuments, these including several to members of the Wroughton family and one to a Col Glanville, who died for his king during the Civil War, which includes not only an alabaster effigy in full armour, but his real armour and an organised death figure in a shroud. **Broad Town**, between these two fine villages, is home to one of Wiltshire's less well-known white horses. It was probably carved in the mid-19th century by a local farmer, whose knowledge of the equine form does not seem to have extended to where the eyes were situated. Though the horse is fading away through lack of care, it can still be discerned. A better-known figure is the horse cut on the side of **Hackpen Hill**, which is crossed by a minor road opposite the turning to Broad Hinton. Though well-known, the horse is quite difficult to see as the hill slope is only 30 degrees, leading to considerable foreshortening. The figure's origins are debated, but most experts favour a cutting in 1838 to celebrate the coronation of Queen Victoria.

Closer to Wootton Bassett, **Lyneham** is famed for its RAF base, from which Hercules aircraft fly regularly on training runs. Visitors may well see the planes: indeed, if they are in the vicinity they can hardly be missed as they fly very low and slowly, blocking out the sun and drowning all other sounds – an impressive sight.

West again are more pretty villages, the most interesting of which are **Bradenstoke** (see feature box), **Christian Malford**, with its interesting church which has 13th-century origins, and **Kington St Michael**, where the **Lyte Almshouses** in the main street were founded in 1675 by Isaac Lyte, a London Alderman. In **Stanton Park**, a short distance south-west of **Stanton St Quintin**, the remains of a Roman villa have been excavated. **Leigh Delamere**, another pleasant village with a fine parsonage and almshouses, is much better known for its name having been acquired for the nearby service area on the M4. On the road from Wooton Bassett to Malmesbury, **Brinkworth** claims to be England's longest village, and as it is over 4 miles (about 6½km) between the village signs on the B4042 that may well be correct.

Malmesbury

Beyond the villages is **Malmesbury**, whose **Abbey** is one of the highlights of a visit to north Wiltshire. The hill site, almost completely surrounded by the waters of the River Avon and Ingleburn (the latter occasionally called the Tetbury Avon), was almost certainly inhabited from earliest times, but recorded history begins with the arrival of Maeldulph, a Celtic hermit, probably in the early years of the 7th century AD. Although Maeldulph was at first the lone occupant of the site, his teachings to those who visited became famous and he eventually started a small school at the site. One of his early pupils was Aldhelm, born into the royal family of Wessex in about AD640. Aldhelm was a brilliant pupil and a great favourite of Maeldulph. Aldhelm left Malmesbury to become a monk at Canterbury in 671. However, his health was poor and he decided to return to Malmesbury. Dates now become a little inconsistent. It is believed that Maeldulph either retired or died in 672 or, perhaps, 675. Some experts have the Celt arriving in Malmesbury as early as AD600 which, if true, suggests he lived to a great age. The sojourn of Aldhelm at Canterbury must also have been very short if he was back at Malmesbury in 671, and his health could not have been as bad as feared as he is thought to have lived

Eilmer, the first aeronaut

If the claim of Icarus is discounted, then Eilmer, an early 11th-century Malmesbury monk, has a strong claim to being the first human bird. At some time during his residency at the abbey (1000–10), Eilmer built wings for his arms and legs and climbed to the top of the abbey tower and hurled himself off. His flapping was a failure, but he did manage to glide about 200 yards. Sadly his landing was more violent than he had intended and he broke both his legs. Undaunted by the failure – he apparently had a permanent limp as a result of the crash – Eilmer was determined to try again, but the abbot forbade further attempts.

Above: Castle Combe

Left: Broad Hinton

Below: Autumn colours at the National Arboretum

The Tolsey Gate

Close to the Market Cross, the Tolsey Gate allows access to the Abbey. It was here that blind houses were located, lock-ups without windows (hence 'blind') into which drunks were thrown to sober up without causing a public nuisance. The idea is believed by some to be the basis of the expression 'blind drunk'. Malmesbury also had stocks near the Market Cross, where persistent offenders were placed. As elsewhere, passing crowds would jeer and throw things. Fruit and eggs are usually cited, but these were expensive and a much cheaper missile – a handful of mud – was much more likely to be used. It is claimed that this is the basis of that other drinking expression – 'mud in your eye'.

until 709.

Whatever the truth of the dates, it is clear that Aldhelm founded the first monastery at Malmesbury. Like his master, Aldhelm was a great teacher, as well as being an accomplished musician (it is claimed his monastery was home to the first organ constructed in England, a 'mighty instrument … blown by bellows') and a miracle-worker, the latter soon making Malmesbury an important pilgrimage centre. In 705 Aldhelm went to Sherborne, Dorset, building the abbey there, but was brought back to Malmesbury for burial.

Malmesbury continued to be important, the town that rose beside it becoming even more prosperous when Alfred the Great made it part of his defensive border against the Norsemen to the north (just as he did with Cricklade). The Norse sacked the town in 877, though they apparently left the monastery intact. The town was quickly retaken and restored, and in the reign of Athelstan – who has a strong claim to having been the first true king of England, though he was never actually crowned as such – was made his capital.

There was a royal mint at the town and when he died, in AD940, Athelstan was buried at the abbey.

Although exact details are lacking, it is likely that the Normans rebuilt the abbey as a Benedictine monastery in the 12th century. At around the same time, one of the most famous of Malmesbury's sons was resident. William of Malmesbury (c.1095–1143) is now recognised as the greatest historian of his time. Half-Saxon, half-Norman, he was apparently an idle monk, much keener on the warm library than the cold rigours of the monastic round. Perhaps it is just as well, because William's efforts to set down Saxon history (as well as tittle-tattle about the Norman conquerors: William would have been a great gossip columnist today) have produced a treasure trove for later historians. He is also responsible for the story of Eilmer the Flying Monk (see feature box).

Over the years of the early medieval period Malmesbury's fortunes rose, to the extent that further abbey buildings were constructed and a massive spire, taller than that on Salisbury Cathedral, was added to the western, and taller, of the two towers. But, as with all other

English monastic buildings, Malmesbury did not survive Henry VIII's Dissolution. As elsewhere, the weather tore at the buildings, stripped of their valuables, bringing about the collapse of the towers by about 1530. The nave of the church was taken over as the parish church while William Stumpe, a cloth weaver, installed looms in some of the outbuildings.

The remaining abbey is a magnificent building, particularly the South Porch, the decoration of which is considered by many to be the finest piece of Norman sculpture in England. Inside there is more excellent decoration, as well as fine memorials and the tomb of King Athelstan. In the churchyard – head towards the Market Cross and it is on your left – is the grave of Hannah Twynnoy who, in 1703, was mauled to death by a tiger which had escaped from a circus. It is ironic that Hannah's death was actually close to the White Lion Inn.

The **Market Cross** is a good place to explore the town once the abbey has been visited. It was built in about 1500 and was considered by Pevsner to be among the finest in England. Leland, the Elizabethan historian, claimed that the octagonal shape was to allow 'poore market folks to stande dry when rayne cummeth'.

Immediately north of the Market Cross, beside the Abbey, are **Abbey House Gardens**. The origins of the house are 13th century, when it formed part of the Abbey complex, but it was extensively remodelled by William Stumpe in 1542. The gardens around the house extend to 5 acres (2 hectares), a remarkable size for the heart of the town. The gardens are the work of Ian and Barbara Pollard, better known among the gardening fraternity as the Naked Gardeners because of their enthusiasm for naturism. The gardens are among the finest in the West of England, with over 10,000 trees, shrubs and plants, among the delights of which are spring's daffodils, the Japanese maples and the herb garden with its pond and fountain.

With your back to the Market Cross, facing High Street, go right to reach the Tourist Information Office, to the right. In the square beyond, beside Cross Hayes, the **Athelstan Museum**, to the right, has an interesting collection exploring local archaeology and history, including items on lace-making, which was a cottage industry in the town in the 18th and 19th centuries. Alternatively from the Cross, turn right along Oxford Street (with the Abbey to your right). To the left is the **White Lion Inn** where poor Hannah Twynnoy died. Now turn right into Gloucester Street. To the right, the 14th-century spire is all that remains of **St Mary's**, the original parish church. Ahead now there is a cobbled strip in the road which marks the position of the old town walls. To the right the **Old Bell Hotel** was built in the 13th century as the Abbey guest house, though later renovated and extended. Beyond, bear right at Westport into St Mary's Street. It is believed that it was here that the political philosopher Thomas Hobbes was born in 1588. Hobbes is most famous for his book *Leviathan*, published in 1651 which established the foundation for most of Western political philosophy. Ahead now is **Horsefair**, with a collection of delightful cottages.

Elsewhere, it is worth heading south from Market Cross, following High Street to reach St John's Street, to the left. On the corner are a superb decorated and inscribed archway and, beside it, **St John's Almshouses**, built in 1694 on the site of the 12th-century St John the Baptist Hospital. The archway was the entrance to the old hospital. To the right here, the River Avon flows over a pair of manmade cataracts.

Around Malmesbury

North-east of Malmesbury is **Charlton Park House**, built on land once owned by the Abbey. The land here formed part of William Stumpe's holding and eventually passed to his great-granddaughter, who married the first Earl of Suffolk. He built the house for her in the early years of the 17th century. The house was much altered over the next 100 years or so, the interior now being a classic example of Georgian, with later modifications. At one time a small section of the ground floor was open to visitors, but now it is only possible to view at times when events are being held.

North again, the church at **Oaksey** is worth visiting for the 15th-century stained glass in one of the northern windows. To the west of the village, right on the border with Gloucestershire, is **Kemble**. The airfield here was once the home of the RAF's Red Arrows display team, their training offering locals a regular chance to see the incredible skill of the pilots. The team has now moved away, but flight enthusiasts will visit to see the collection of engines, aircraft and missiles which trace the history of the Bristol Aeroplane Company. The **Delta Jets Collection** at the site is a collection of vintage jet aircraft which are being carefully restored. The collection can be visited by prior arrangement.

West of Malmesbury are villages which are outliers of the Cotswolds, sharing with the area's more famous towns and villages a wealth of cottages in distinctive Cotswold stone, with cleaved stone tiles on the roofs. **Easton Grey** is the best: there is a fine Georgian mansion and an arched bridge over the River Avon. **Sherston** is associated with the legend of John Rattlebones, who, with Edmund Ironsides, is said to have defeated the Danes near here in 1016. The church contains an effigy known as Rattlebones, but as it is Norman, it is far more likely to be a saint than a Saxon general.

West of the two villages – and over the county boundary in Gloucestershire – is the **National Arboretum** at **Westonbirt**, and few visitors will miss the opportunity of visiting what has been claimed as the finest collection of trees in the world, with over 3,000 varieties, including some which are very rare and endangered in their native countries. The arboretum extends over 600 acres (240 hectares) and includes unusual trees such as the redwood. Although the specimen here does not approach the height of those in California, it does give some idea of the spectacular nature of those giants. The tree has a very strange bark, not hard as on most British trees but soft and fibrous, and a rich chestnut in colour. The arboretum was set up by Robert Holford, whose alabaster effigy can be seen in the church at the nearby village of Westonbirt, and is now managed by the Forestry Commission. Visitors in the autumn are assured of one of the most colourful sights in the Cotswolds, especially when the acers change colour, while those who come in the spring can see a spectacular show of rhododendrons and azaleas.

South of Westonbirt, and also over the county boundary, is the village of **Great Badminton**, which sits beside one of the most famous estates in Britain, the Beaufort. The name Badminton is famous throughout the world in two sports: the game named from the estate; and the three-day event, one of the world's foremost horse trials. The house is 17th century and a very fine example of this period. The interior is rich in decoration, some of it unique. The house stands in over 15,000 acres (6,000 hectares) of park and estate land – the total estate being nearly 10 miles (16km) around. The park is partly natural, partly the work of Capability Brown, and partly formal. One of the more formal aspects, the Great Avenue running down from Worcester Lodge and the A433 near Didmarton, is several miles long and contains thousands of trees. Within the park are deer herds and several excellent follies. The house is occasionally open during the summer months. Local Tourist Offices will have details.

South again and across the M4, the church at **West Kington** is set on a hill, its tower thus set off to perfection. Inside is a pulpit that was used by Hugh Latimer while he was rector here, before becoming Bishop of Worcester. Latimer

Dr Doolittle at Castle Combe

Despite being far from the sea, when it was decided to film Dr Doolittle with Rex Harrison, Castle Combe's picturesque qualities won out over villages with the clear head-start of actually being on the coast. By Brook, which runs through the lower village, and cottages close to it were transformed by the magic of the motion picture industry into a port – a very convincing one.

was executed by burning with Nicholas Ridley, Bishop of London, at Oxford, when they refused to accept Catholicism after the accession of Queen Mary Tudor. Panels to these two martyrs are among those at **Little Sodbury**.

Nearby is arguably the most famous of Wiltshire's villages, **Castle Combe**. It is set in a valley, sheltered and secluded, and has been used as a film location for period dramas. The wealth of the village was based on sheep, as everywhere in the region, but Castle Combe had a charter to hold a fair, where sheep and wool changed hands, as well as other market goods. It was 'the most celebrated faire in North Wiltshire for sheep … whither sheep-masters doe come as far as from Northamptonshire'. To the north of the village there are the remains of the Norman castle built by one of the early lords of the manor.

A memorial to this lord, Walter de Dunstanville, is in the church, a fine tomb with an effigy of the knight in a full suit of chain mail. The rest of the church is good, though extensive late-19th-century restoration was not entirely satisfactory. For such a wealthy village, the church is not automatically recognisable as a wool church although the tower, erected by local clothiers, is more elaborate than might be expected. The market cross stands at the village centre, covered by a roof on four pillars. To the west the restored **Manor House**, now a hotel, dates originally from the 17th century, as does **Dower House** to the north. One Lord of the Manor in the 14th century, Sir John Fastolf, is thought to have been Shakespeare's model for Falstaff. Those interested in discovering more of the history of the village – which claims to be the prettiest in England, and would almost certainly make the top ten of everyone's list – should visit the museum in **Combe**

Cottage. A rather more adrenalin-fuelled visit can be made to the racing circuit east of the village, which hosts a number of events through the year. There is a racing school at the circuit where budding drivers can learn their trade. On 'classic' days classic cars and motorbikes are on display and in action, and visitors may even take their own cars onto the circuit.

To the east of Castle Combe is **Yatton Keynell**. Keynell was added to the village's name by the lords of the manor who had the name. One of the earliest members of the family, Sir William, built the original church on this site: it was dedicated to St Margaret of Antioch as a gesture of thanks for his safe return from the Crusades.

Places to Visit

Cricklade

Cotswold Water Park/Keynes Country Park

Open: All year, but individual facilities have different times and some are closed during the winter months. Ring for details.
☎ 01285 861459

Town Museum

16 Calcutt Street, Cricklade
Open: All year Sat 10am–12 noon. Also open Apr–Sep, Wed 2–4pm and on Sat and Sun 2–4pm during Jul & Aug.
☎ 01793 750686

Purton Museum

1 High Street, Purton
Open: All year, Tue and Fri 2–5pm and 6–8pm, Wed 10am–1pm, 2–5pm.
☎ 01793 770928

Swindon and Cricklade Railway

Blunsdon Station
Tadpole Lane, Blunsdon
Open: All year, daily 11am–4pm. Trains operate Sat and Sun y 11am–4pm. Steam trains operate on Sundays from Easter–October, and on special event days – call for details.
☎ 01793 771615

Places to Visit

Swindon

Swindon Museum and Art Gallery

Bath Road, Swindon
Open: All year, Mon–Sat 10am–5pm.
Closed Sun and Bank Holidays.
☎ 01793 466556

STEAM (Museum of the Great Western Railway)

Kemble Drive, Swindon
Open: All year, daily 10am–5pm.
Closed Christmas Day, Boxing Day
and New Year's Day.
☎ 01793 466646

Great Western Designer Outlet

Kemble Drive, Swindon
Open: All year, Mon, Tue, Wed and
Fri 10am–6pm, Thu 10am–8pm, Sat
9am–6pm, Sun 11am–5pm. Closed
or open for limited periods at Bank
Holidays.
☎ 01793 507600

National Monuments Records Centre

Kemble Drive, Swindon
Open: All year, Mon–Fri 9.30am
–5pm. Closed on Bank Holidays.
☎ 01793 414600

Museum of Computing

University of Bath in Swindon, Oakfield
Campus, Marlowe Avenue, Swindon
Open: All year, Mon–Fri 10am–4pm,
Sat 1am–1pm. Closed on Bank
Holidays.
☎ 07834 375628 or 07939 582544

Butterfly World

Studley Grange Garden and
Leisure Park Hay Lane, Wroughton
Open: All year, daily except
Christmas Day, 10am–6pm (Sun
5pm) or dusk. Last admission
30 minutes before closing.
☎ 01793 852400

Science Museum Swindon

Hackpen Lane, Wroughton
Open: Regular programme of open
days and special events. Please ring
for details.
☎ 01793 846200

Richard Jefferies House and Museum

Coate
Open: All year, second Wed of the
month 10am–4pm. Also open on
the first and third Sun of each month
from May to Sep, 2–5pm. Admission
free.
☎ 01793 783040

Coate Water Country Park

Open: The Park is open at any
reasonable time, but facilities are, in
general open all year Mon–Fri 10am–
dusk, Sat and Sun 9am–dusk.
☎ 01793 490150

Lydiard Park

Lydiard Tregoze
Open: House and Walled Garden: All
year Tue–Sun 11am–5pm (4pm from
Nov to Feb). Closed 24–26 Dec. Park:
All year, daily dawn–dusk.
☎ 01793 770401

Roves Farm

Sevenhampton, Highworth
Open: mid-Feb–early Nov, Wed–Sun 10.30am–5.00pm, but daily in Jun, Jul and school holidays, same times.
☎ 01793 763939

Wootton Bassett

Town Museum

High Street
Open: All year, Sat 10.30am–12noon. Closed at Christmas and New Year.
☎ 01793 537489

Malmesbury

Malmesbury Abbey

Open: All year (including all Bank Holidays), daily 10am–5pm (4pm Nov–Mar).
☎ 01666 826666

Abbey House Gardens

Open: Late Mar–late Oct, daily 11am–5.30pm.
☎ 01666 822212

Athelstan Museum

Town Hall, Cross Hayes
Open: All year, daily 10.30am–4.30pm (11.30am–3.30pm Nov–Mar).
☎ 01666 829258

Charlton Park House

Upper Minety
Open: Only for special events. Ask at Malmesbury Tourist office for details.

Bristol Aero Collection

Kemble Airfield
(Entry at main gate on the A429)
Open: All year Mon 10am–4pm. Closed at Christmas and New Year. Also open on Sun and Bank Holidays from Easter to October, same times.
☎ 01285 771204 (during open times only).

Delta Jets Collection

Kemble Airfield
Open: by prior arrangement only.
☎ 01285 771177

National Arboretum

Westonbirt
Open: Apr–Nov, Mon–Fri 9am–8pm or dusk. Sat and Sun 8am–8pm or dusk. Also open on special evenings in autumn when there is a full moon.
☎ 01666 880220

Castle Combe

Village Museum

Combe Cottage
Open: Easter–Oct, Sun and Bank Holidays 2–5pm.
☎ 01249 782250

Racing Circuit

Open: Annual calendar of events – ring for details – and a racing school.
☎ 01249 782417

To the west of the county are a series of towns which grew prosperous from the wool of downland sheep. Here, too, are fine houses – one with an important part in the history of photography – and a steep village with one of England's best Saxon churches. A quick detour into Somerset adds a visit to Britain's finest Georgian city.

South of Yatton Keynell (see Chapter 1) there is a final section of wold, the high pasture for sheep grazing which was the source of the prosperity of the Cotswolds. At its centre is Biddestone, the old village houses a reminder of the warm Cotswold stone, set in a true Cotswold landscape. To the west, Slaughterford was probably given its name to distinguish the ford near the sloe trees from another ford, to the north, rather than as a memorial to a bloody, but now forgotten, battle. East of Biddestone is Sheldon Manor. The manor is one of the oldest houses in Wiltshire, dating in part from the 13th century, and has been continuously lived in for nearly 700 years. Its 13th-century porch was described as astounding by Pevsner (though he considered it much too large for the house). Today the manor stands in splendid isolation, but it was once part of a village, long abandoned and lost. The Manor gardens are a mix of the formal and informal: the rose garden is particularly good. A 15th-century chapel stands in the gardens.

Chippenham

A short distance east of Sheldon Manor is **Chippenham**. The origins of the town's name are still debated. 'Chipping' is the old name for a market and is the prefix for many town and village names throughout the country – including several local ones – as well as being the origin of Cheapside in London. Hamme refers to low-lying land near a river bend. So 'the market by the river bend' – but some disagree, believing the first part of the name to be from a Saxon called Cyppa who owned this particular piece of land. During the conflict between the Norse and the Saxons over what is now Wiltshire, Chippenham was the Norse base when they were in the ascendancy after winning a battle at the town in 877. Then, after the battle at Edington, to the east of Westbury, the following year the Saxons regained control and Chippenham was for a time King Alfred's residence.

The town's site was not ideal, the river flooding regularly, to the annoyance of both the townspeople and the local traders, who were denied access to a lucrative market. The problem was partially solved in the late 15th century when Maud Heath, the widow of a market trader, who lived at **East Tytherton** to the east of the town, handed over rents from local land and property to build and maintain a causeway from Wick Hill through East Tytherton and Langley Burrell, crossing the River Avon along the way, to Chippenham. For most of the route the causeway is no more than a raised path, but in the low-lying section it is a true causeway and there it can still be seen. The best remaining section is at **Kellaways**, where 64 arches lifted the causeway above the flood plain. In 1833 a memorial to Maud was erected on **Wick Hill**, Maud herself being depicted in shawl and bonnet. In 1974 a sundial was erected at East Tytherton to commemorate the causeway's 500th anniversary.

The Chippenham end of **Maud Heath's Causeway** is marked with a plate. To that simple memorial has been added a series of plaques around the town which note the sites of important events or places in the town's history. One on 56 St Mary's Street notes the fighting which took place there during the Civil War when Royalists attacked the Parliament-held town. Another, at 4a High Street, notes that the town's cheese market was the most important in the West of England, with 1,856 tons of cheese sold in 1872. Most of the plaques are to be found close to the Market Place and in High Street.

Market Place is the best place to start a tour of the town. The old **Butter Cross** – actually a stone roof supported by six pillars – was removed to Castle Combe manor house in 1889, but eventually returned to its rightful place in 1996. Close by, the **Angel Hotel**, a fine Georgian building, is one of the town's oldest coaching inns. Beside it is the **Museum and Heritage Centre**, where visitors can learn more of Chippenham's history. Also in Market Place is **Yelde Hall**, one of the town's oldest buildings. Built in the 16th century, initially as a Court House and Town Hall, the Hall was the centre of an area known as the Shambles (part of the market – the word originally meant a slaughterhouse, the present usage for something poorly organized deriving from the entrails of slaughtered animals being left all over the place) and became engulfed by other buildings. Several of the buildings which hemmed in the Hall were removed some years ago and the building was restored for use as a museum. It is now the town's Tourist Information Office.

From Market Place a walk along High Street is worthwhile, but be sure to look at the fine buildings in St Mary's Street. Across the River Avon are the arches of the bridge which carried Brunel's GWR to London. Before the construction of Box Tunnel, the GWR finished at Chippenham and Rowland Brotherhood, one of Brunel's engineers, set up a works here to build signals, points, bridges and wagons. The works were important, bringing much-needed employment and prosperity to the town. Brunel also built houses close to the viaduct for directors of the GWR. These were demolished some years ago to allow construction of a modern office block. Those who knew the old

Chippenham People

Robert Peel (1788–1850) was elected MP for Chippenham in 1812, though his term was short as he was elected as MP for Oxford in 1817. As Home Secretary in the 1820s Peel was responsible for the setting-up of the Metropolitan Police and is the origin of the names 'Bobby' and 'Peeler' for a policeman. Peel was Prime Minister on two occasions, 1834–5 and 1835–41.

Francis Kilvert (1840–79), the famous diarist, was born at Langley Burrell where his father, Robert, was rector. He was educated at Wadham College, Oxford (at the same time as Charles Dodgson – Lewis Carroll – was there), then entered the Church, initially as curate to his father. He later moved to various parishes in the Welsh Marches. Kilvert's diaries are a valuable source of information on rural life in late-19th-century England and Wales, and though they are most famous for the entries from his time in the Marches they also include sections on life around Chippenham. Each year the Kilvert Society holds a service in his honour at St Peter's, Langley Burrell.

The association of rock 'n' roller **Eddie Cochran** (1938–60) with Chippenham was brief and fatal. During a British tour Cochrane had performed in Bristol and was being taken back to London in a Ford Consul taxi, together with his girlfriend Sharon Sheeley and fellow performer Gene Vincent. At 11.50pm on the evening of 16 April 1960 the taxi collided with a lamp post on the A4 at Rowden Hill. Cochrane was taken to hospital at Bath, but was pronounced dead at 4am the following morning. Both Sharon Sheeley and Gene Vincent were badly injured in the accident. The taxi driver was subsequently found guilty of dangerous driving, imprisoned for 6 months and banned from driving for 15 years. A plaque marks the spot where the accident occurred and is still visited by fans of Cochran's short career.

houses claim that the change left the town considerably poorer in terms of architectural elegance. A superior piece of architecture is the **Wiltshire and Swindon History Centre** in Cocklebury Road (about 250 yards (230m) from the railway station), where people researching their county ancestors, or aspects of county history, can find information and advice.

South of Chippenham

South of Chippenham – take the A350 for Melksham – is **Lackham Country Park**, the grounds of Wiltshire College which now occupies the site's imposing late-Georgian house. The **Museum of Agriculture and Rural Life** is housed in preserved farm buildings on the College campus, the collection includ-

West Wiltshire: Wool towns and the Avon Valley

Below: Bowood House

Right: Beautiful Rhododendron flower in full bloom

Map labels:
- A420
- Biddestone
- Museum
- History Centre
- Chippenham
- A4
- A3102
- Heritage Centre
- Motor Museum
- Compton Basset
- Corsham Court
- Sheldon Manor
- Lackham Gardens
- Bowood House
- Calne
- A4
- Cherhill
- A46
- Box
- A4
- Corsham
- Almshouses
- B3353
- Lacock
- Lacock Abbey
- Sandy Lane
- A342
- Cherhill White Horse
- A363
- A365
- A350
- A365
- A361
- Bath
- A36
- B3109
- Great Chalfield Manor
- Melksham
- Brewery (and Museum Heritage Centre)
- Bishops Cannings
- Barton Farm
- Museum
- B3107
- A365
- A342
- B3110
- Ilford Manor
- Bradford-on-Avon
- Broadleas Gardens
- Devizes
- Westwood Manor

Scale: 0 5 m / 0 5 km

N W E S

ing various old tractors, steam engines and other farming implements, as well as audio-visual and video presentations on aspects of Wiltshire's history. The Country Park has gardens, a self-guided woodland walk, domestic livestock and a colony of meerkats, and miniature train and trailer rides for younger children. There is also an annual programme of special events.

South again is **Lacock**. The village is pleasant and has a church dedicated to St Cyriac, one of only a handful of such dedications in England. The church is interesting, but for most visitors it is the **Abbey** which is the reason for the visit. It was founded in 1232 by Ela, dowager Countess of Salisbury as an Augustinian nunnery. The Countess also founded Hinton Charterhouse, across the county boundary in Somerset. She retired to Lacock as its first abbess. The Abbey was dissolved in 1539 and bought by Sir William Sharington (whose impressive memorial can be seen in St Cyriac's Church. Of the original Abbey several sections remain, most importantly the cloisters. With the vaulted ceiling and tracery windows they are exquisite. Sharington demolished the Abbey church and some other sections when he converted the buildings into a family home. He also added an octagonal tower, the only part of his remodelling to have survived completely intact. Sharington also added an outer courtyard and a brewery.

Sharington's niece married a member of the Talbot family, a later member of which was William Henry Fox Talbot (see feature box). Talbot did restoration work of his own, including the addition of three oriel windows, one of which has become famous in the history of photography. The Abbey's grounds include a 19th-century woodland garden and a grotto which is all that remains of an 18th-century water garden. W H Fox Talbot was interested in botany as well as photography and his botanical garden is currently being restored.

East from Chippenham the A4 heads towards Calne and soon reaches the entrance to **Bowood House**. The House has a curious history, having begun as a modest dwelling (by the standards of stately homes) in 1725 when constructed by Sir Orlando Bridgeman, then expanding as later owners, the Lansdowne family, who acquired it in 1754, added sections. A new building was added, and then connected to the original house by Robert Adam, the foremost British architect of the late 18th century. Then, in 1955, the process was reversed as parts of the house were demolished. What remains is impressive, and retains much of the better work of the past. Inside, the decoration and furnishings are terrific. There are fine paintings, sculptures and tapestries, Queen Victoria's wedding chair, an important jewellery collection and, somewhat bizarrely, Napoleon's death mask. One fascinating room is Joseph Priestley's laboratory. Priestley (1733–1804) was employed at Bowood as tutor to the Marquess of Lansdowne's son, and carried out his own experiments in his spare time. It was at Bowood that he discovered oxygen, the work for which he is famous. His laboratory is much as it was in his day.

But for all the brilliance of the House, it is the **parkland** surrounding it which

The Fox Talbot Museum

William Henry Fox Talbot was born on 11 February 1800, the only child of William Dempster Talbot, then the occupier of Lacock Abbey. He was educated at Harrow and Cambridge and was a very bright man with several papers on mathematics and optics to his name. Fox Talbot became interested in photography, which was then in its infancy. Early photographic processes involved positive images being produced directly, but the process took many hours. The Frenchman Louis Daguerre had refined the process so that images could be produced more speedily, but the problem was still that a positive image was produced directly so that reproduction of the image was not possible. Fox Talbot solved this problem, creating the first negative/positive process and so allowing multiple images to be formed. His process was also much quicker and cheaper, which meant that rather than being available only to professional photographers, who invariably took portraits for rich clients, amateurs and the less well-off could enjoy photography.

Problems arose over Fox Talbot's patenting of his invention and his sale of licences to use it. His reason for the patent, and his pursuit of those who infringed it, was based on the amount of his own money which he had spent developing the process. However, it was the patent which caused great antagonism. In 1854, a year before Fox Talbot's patent was due to expire, and after he had applied for a 14-year renewal, his claim of infringement against the photographer Martin Laroche failed when Laroche successfully argued that the Fox Talbot process was similar to (though not the same as) another invented by Joseph Reade. Though there were in fact significant differences, his case against Laroche was thrown out and Fox Talbot did not renew his patent.

Fox Talbot's first known photograph produced by his new process was of one of the oriel windows he had installed in Lacock Abbey. The photograph was taken in 1835, four years before he registered his patent.

The museum to his achievements, housed in a medieval barn, explains Fox Talbot's work and process. The upper floor of the barn has a changing programme of work by contemporary and early photographers.

is the great prize of Bowood. The 1,000 acres (400 hectares) were worked on by both Lancelot 'Capability' Brown and Humphry Repton and are magnificent, the whole set off by formal gardens and a huge lake. The **Rhododendron Walk** attracts visitors from across Europe when in flower. For younger children there is a soft play area, those slightly older and more adventurous graduating to the adventure playground which includes a life-size pirate ship. The estate also has a golf course often claimed to be the best in the West of England.

Visitors to Bowood should also head south to the village of **Sandy Lane**, a charming collection of stone and thatch cottages grouped around a thatched church. The cottages were built to accommodate Bowood estate workers whose original cottages were submerged when the lake was created.

Calne

A short distance east along the A4 from Bowood is **Calne**. As with other towns in this area of Wiltshire, Calne grew up in Saxon times, a defensive town on the border between Saxon Wessex and the Norsemen to the north. It is likely that there were earlier settlers, the name probably deriving from the Celtic for the town's position at the confluence of the River Marden and Abberd Brook. In the early medieval period the town was a centre for the woollen industry, clothing maintaining its fortunes until the 19th century when the collapse of the trade brought hard times.

Salvation came, here as elsewhere in Wiltshire, in the form of pigs. In the days before refrigeration meat had to be delivered 'on the hoof' and the route of the A4 was then a drovers' road, cattle, sheep and pigs being driven along it to the meat markets of London. One local family saw the advantage of processing the pigs locally; soon the Harris name became famous for bacon, sausages and pies, and Harris' works dominated Calne's economy for 200 years until closing in 1983. The closure was a significant blow to the town, but it has recovered well, its confidence in the future clear from the superb series of public artworks which have been commissioned. Visitors wishing to discover more about the history of the town should seek out the **Calne Heritage Centre** in New Road.

To explore Calne, start at **Bank House**, the Tourist Information Office, set where The Strand meets New Road. Opposite the office is the **Town Hall**, built in the 1880s. Facing it, turn right to reach Bank Row, on the right. Opposite is the site of the Harris factory, now occupied by good modern buildings. This is one of the centres for the public artworks, several pieces being placed outside. Two of the more interesting pieces are *The Head*, by Rick Kirby, and the bronze relief by Vivien ap Rhys Pryce. The latter illustrates Jan Ingenhousz (1730–99) who was, like Priestley, a tutor at Bowood House. Ingenhousz was also a formidable scientist: he was the first to note Brownian motion and suggested the use of live smallpox virus in inoculations before Edward Jenner developed his much safer technique using cowpox virus as a vaccine. Ingenhousz is buried in Calne churchyard.

Those interested in the artworks can obtain a leaflet from the Tourist Office with their locations. Everyone will have their own favourite – for me it is the **Two Pigs** by Richard Cowdy, which can be seen in Phelps Parade, reached by continuing along The Strand then bearing right into High Street, turning right at its end and then, soon after, turning right again.

Continue along Bank Row, with the river to your right. Further along the river there is a spot called **Doctor's Pond**, where, it is said, Joseph Priestley conducted experiments, though the nature of these is sadly lost. From Bank

Row turn right into Church Street, passing **Butcher's Row** to the left. It is believed the name is medieval, though the present buildings date from the 18th and 19th centuries, the time when the Harris family were taking an interest in drove animals passing through the town. **St Mary's Church**, beyond the Row, has Norman origins and is very large for the size of the settlement at the time of its construction (it was completed by 1155). So large is it in comparison to other local churches that it has often been called the 'Cathedral of North Wiltshire'. Just beyond are **Dr Tounson's Almshouses**, built in 1682 by the vicar of Bremhill for elderly widows.

At the bottom of Church Street a left turn reaches **The Green**, a delightful memory of the medieval period when Calne was a small weaving town, rather than the more bustling place it is now. One of the houses close to the green is still called The Weaver's House, though this is a misnomer as it more likely housed carding and spinning machinery. Turning right from Church Street you soon reach **Marden House**, over to the left. Once the home of the manager of the local wharf on the **Wilts and Berks Canal**, the house now plays host to a regular programme of Sunday music recitals. The canal was built between 1795 and 1810 and connected the Kennet and Avon Canal near Melksham to the Thames and Severn Canal at Cricklade. It brought coal to Calne from the Somerset coalfields, as well as other materials, but it had a short life: by 1840 railways were signalling the end of the canal era. The Wilts and Berks continued until the 1860s, when the local railways virtually ended trade. In 1901 the Stanley Aqueduct, between Chippenham and Calne, collapsed, ending the canal's usefulness and it was abandoned. Now, as elsewhere,

The Witan of 978

Witan is Saxon for a meeting. The term is actually a short form for *wienagemot*, that word also giving us moot. Moots were local gatherings to discuss things of common interest. They were held at specific sites – moot points, which explains today's usage. Witans were more formal, usually councils of local lords or bishops to discuss matters of state. In 978 a witan was held at Calne to discuss St Dunstan's view that the clergy should be celibate. Dunstan was Archbishop of Canterbury and so his opinion carried considerable weight, but there were many in the audience who disagreed with him. The witan was held in a building which, unusually for the time, was two-storey, and the council was in the upper room. As Dunstan spoke in favour of his proposal, the floor of the room collapsed. Many of the council were killed or injured, but Dunstan happened to have been standing on a cross-beam and was left safe if, presumably, shaken. The surviving members of the council saw Dunstan's survival as miraculous, an indication of God's agreement with the Archbishop's position, and clerical celibacy was adopted.

The Cherhill horse

the canal is being restored; it is a slow process, but the intention is to reopen the entire length. Those interested in the canal can follow a section by going west from the junction of Station Road and New Road.

Heading east from Calne centre, a right turn into Stockley Lane (just after the Talbot Inn) reaches the **Atwell–Wilson Motor Museum**, a collection of over 100 vintage and classic cars, motorcycles and commercial vehicles dating from the 1920s through to more recent classics.

East of Calne

Continuing east the visitor soon encounters another of Wiltshire's white horses. The **Cherhill horse**, on the down to the south-east of the village, was cut in 1780 by men working for Dr Christopher Alsop of Calne. Alsop had the horse cut for no better reason than that he wanted to. In Calne he was known as the 'Mad Doctor'

– though whether this was before or after the cutting is not clear. If before, he lived up to the title by controlling the cutting from the road, bellowing out instructions through a megaphone. In its original form the horse's eye – a significant feature more than four feet (over a metre) across – was made of bottles buried neck-first into the chalk so that their upturned bottoms sparkled in the sun.

The horse, which is about 125 feet (38m) long and 130 feet (40m) high, stands just below the ramparts of **Oldbury Castle**, a double ditch/rampart Iron Age hillfort. The monument at the fort's western edge was erected in the early 1840s by Lord Lansdown as a memorial to his ancestor Sir William Petty, the 17th-century economist. The downland beyond the hillfort and monument, particularly **Calstone Down**, is superb walking country. The Down, reached along Ranscombe Bottom from the hamlet of **Calstone Wellington** is a wonderfully

The Cherhill Highwaymen

In the 18th century Cherhill was infamous as the home of a gang of highwaymen who robbed travellers on the A4's forerunner, the coach road from Bath to London. It is said that the gang attacked travellers in the nude (the robbers not the robbed) on the grounds that they were more likely to be recognised by their clothes than their faces. If true, this would seem to qualify the Cherhill gang as the most eccentric highwaymen in history. Architecturally Cherhill village has nothing as exotic as its naked robbers, its finest building, a huge medieval tithe barn with a slated roof, having been demolished in the 1950s.

folded landscape. The hamlet's church is delightfully set on the slopes of the down above a small reservoir.

Calstone Down leads to **North Down** (more easily reached from a car park at the top of a minor road heading south from Calne), which is crossed by the **Wansdyke**. The Wansdyke is the longest earthwork of its kind in Britain, linking Dundry Hill in northern Somerset to Hampshire, a distance of 50 miles (80km), though it is no longer continuous (and may never have been along its entire length). The dyke is a ditch with a bank on its southern side and is believed to date from either the late Romano-British period, perhaps built to keep out the Saxons as a final

rearguard action, or by the Saxons themselves as a border between Mercia and Wessex. The name is certainly Saxon, from Woden's Dyke. To the west of the car park the dyke is not continuous, though there is a Roman road, but to the east, from Morgan's Hill, it is, and can be followed to Marlborough and beyond.

Beyond the car park and the nearby golf course is **Roundway Down**. The Down was the scene, in 1643, of a major Civil War battle. After the Parliamentarian army of Sir William Waller had been forced to yield Bath to the Royalists it regrouped on the Down. On 13 July the Royalist army under Sir Ralph Hopton arrived opposite Waller's force. Each army occupied a ridge, separated by a shallow depression. Waller's cavalry charged the Royalists, but the slight counter-gradient was too much for the horses carrying the heavily armoured troops. Their charge faltered and, sensing their chance, the Royalist cavalry charged. Waller's cavalry was routed and his infantry, confronted by enemy cavalry, and, behind them, the Cornish infantry who had given them a hiding at Lansdown, near Bath, turned and fled. Waller lost 600 dead, 1,000 captured and almost all his artillery: his army was effectively destroyed. It is said that each year, on the anniversary of the battle, the cries of the dying can be heard echoing across the field.

South of Roundway Down, **Bishops Cannings** has a strong claim to being the true home of the **Moonrakers** of the legend (see Introduction), though the pond in question was probably Crammer Pond near Devizes. The first part of the village's name is from the

Bishop of Salisbury who 'owned' it in medieval times, this probably explaining the size, wealth and design of the village church. Its 130ft (40m) spire is a local landmark. Inside there is a curious seat, its back painted with a huge black hand on which are inscribed, in Latin, references to death and sin. The church organ was donated by a local man who, as a cabin boy, circumnavigated the world with Captain Cook.

Devizes

From Bishops Cannings it is a short distance west to **Devizes**. There is evidence of prehistoric and Roman settlements close to the town site, but history really begins with the building of a castle by the Normans in about 1080. The first castle was destroyed by fire, but a second one was claimed to be one of the strongest in the country, a claim backed up by the decision of King John to use it to store the Crown Jewels when a French invasion was feared. With more peaceful times, the castle fell into disrepair, its demolition being completed when the locals used it as a convenient building stone quarry after it had been slighted by the Parliamentarians during the Civil War. The present castle, south-west of the Market Place, dates from the mid-19th century. The town's fortunes rose after the setback of the Civil War, Devizes becoming a centre for the wool trade as well as an important market town. After the wool trade boom of the 17th and 18th centuries, the arrival of the Kennet and Avon Canal in 1810 further boosted the town's fortunes. Ultimately, the ending of the wool trade and the end of the canal era brought a

The name Devizes

The town's curious name derives from its position at the point where three parishes met. Two of these – Potterne and Rowde – were owned by the King, while Cannings was owned by the Bishop of Salisbury. The town therefore sat ad divisas, at the boundaries. That position almost certainly helped the town's market become one of the most significant locally.

slow decline, but the town has coped well, integrating the needs of a modern community with a wealth of historic buildings rather better than many other places of similar size.

Those wanting to explore the town should start in **Market Place**, which

May God strike me dead...

A plaque on the Market Cross tells the story of Ruth Pierce, a housewife from Potterne who visited Devizes market on 25 January 1753 with three friends. The four women agreed to buy a sack of grain between them, but when the money was counted out it was threepence short. The other three women insisted that it was Ruth Pierce who had not paid her full share. When confronted Mrs Pierce called on God to strike her dead if she had not paid her full share. Called on to repeat this oath she did so – and promptly fell down dead, the threepence still clutched in her hand.

Caen Hill Locks

The Kennet and Avon Canal was engineered by John Rennie. Canals were authorised by Act of Parliament, in this case by an Act of 1794. It took 16 years to complete the 87 miles (140km) from Bristol to Reading; a long time, but it must be recalled that the canal was entirely dug by hand, by teams of navigators. The name of these hardy men is the root of 'navvy', the now impolite name for those who do manual labour. At Caen Hill it was necessary to lift the canal 237ft (72m) from the Avon valley to Devizes. Rennie accomplished this with a series of 29 locks over a distance of 2½ miles (4km), with 16 of them very close together, almost forming a linear staircase with associated ponds for holding water. The ponds are a haven for wildlife. The locks were dug from a clay soil, the vast quantity of clay forming the basis of a local brick-making industry.

has often been called the best in the West of England. With its array of fine buildings it is easy to see why. The inns where the more important traders lodged survive, while the old **Market House** (known locally as The Shambles) is still a market.

Close to Market Place is **Wadworth's Northgate Brewery** (several deep breaths are a better guide to location than any directions), where 6X and other famous beers are brewed. Shire horses still pull a cask-laden cart through the town, and the horses can be visited at the brewery site. There is also a reception centre with beer and souvenirs for sale.

From Market Place Snuff Street – in which a snuff factory once stood – leads north to New Park Street. Ahead, in Couch Lane, is the museum of the **Kennet and Avon Canal Trust**, which explores the history of the canal. The canal opened in 1810, but, as with all other waterways, was effectively closed by the arrival of the railways less than 30 years later. The importance of the old canal, and the beauty of the

route it took – passing through such historically important cities and towns as Bristol, Bath, Devizes, Newbury and Reading – meant that its restoration became a prestigious project for British Waterways, local authorities and the Canal Trust. Aided by a grant from the National Lottery the canal has been completely rehabilitated and is now navigable again, its towpath a joy for walkers and cyclists. The canal also has, at **Caen Hill**, a little way west of Devizes, one of Britain's most audacious sections of waterway engineering (see feature box).

Turning left along New Park Street the visitor soon reaches **St Mary's Church**. Devizes is curious in having two fine Norman churches, this being the less spectacular of them. There are further interesting buildings in Monday Market Street and the adjacent Maryport Street, and **Crammer Pond**, where the Moonrakers hid their booty, is easily reached from here, bearing left along Sidmouth and Estcourt streets.

Devizes' other Norman church is **St John's**, reached by following St

John's Street from the southern side of Market Place. St John's is a beautiful church with a fine 15th-century tower. Across from the church is **Wiltshire Heritage**, which includes a museum of local archaeology and history, an art gallery with county-related works and frequent exhibitions, and a library of local books and manuscripts. Close to the church, **St John's Alley** is one of the most picturesque spots in town, with timber-framed buildings dating from the 16th century.

One last place will be of interest to those wanting to spot all the Wiltshire white horses. On **Roundway Hill**, north-east of the town (follow the A361 towards Swindon, then turn left along Folly Road, then bear right), a new white horse was cut to commemorate the new millennium.

Before heading west from Devizes, a detour south is worthwhile to see **Broadleas Gardens**, a 10-acre (4-hectare) site reminiscent of a Cornish Garden, with camellias, azaleas and rhododendrons, and a host of spring bulbs. Further on, at **Potterne**, **St Mary's Church** is one of the finest in the county, in almost pure Early English style. This is explained by the site being owned by the Bishops of Salisbury, who had the finances to complete the building all at one time, many other parish churches being built over periods of many tens, even hundreds, of years. Apart from some minor later work, the entire church dates from the 13th century.

West of Devizes

Follow the A361 west from Devizes. The main road goes through the extremely pretty village of **Seend**, with its array of fine houses, to reach

St John's Alley, Devizes

Caen Hill Locks

Trowbridge, but we bear right on the A365, crossing the Kennet and Avon Canal to reach Melksham.

Melksham is another Wiltshire market town, with a later history of wool trade prosperity. When the trade declined the town flourished on the stagecoach trade, as it was an important staging post on the journey from Bristol, Bath and the towns of Devon and Cornwall to London. There was also an attempt to turn a spring found to the south of the town into a spa to rival Bath, a grandiose idea which resulted in some speculative building but ultimately failed. The Great Western Railway (GWR) also brought some prosperity as there was a railway works at the town. After the works closed, Melksham was home to several small engineering companies, one of which, the Cooper Tire and Rubber Company Europe (the name taking the American spelling of tyre) is now the town's largest employer, its best known brand being Avon tyres. The most interesting part of the town is that close to the **Market Place**, though the **Conigre Mead Nature Reserve**, on the south side of the River Avon near the A350 bridge, is a very pleasant area. A new walk, inaugurated as part of the millennium celebrations, follows the river from the Reserve.

North-west of Melksham is **Corsham**, a charming town which repays all the time spent in it. It is likely that the name is Saxon, and there was certainly a Saxon presence as Ethelred the Unready had a Manor House here which he used when hunting in the nearby forest. The manor was held by successive monarchs and lords until 1745, when Paul Methuen bought it (see Corsham Court below). As in nearby towns, the wool trade made Corsham prosperous, though here the town's wealth was boosted by quarrying, the famous Bath Stone, a form of Cotswold limestone, being justly famous as a building stone. With the opening of the GWR, the stone could be exported further afield, which led to a rapid development of quarrying. Interestingly, local stone workings were underground rather than the 'opencast' quarries more usually associated with the northern Cotswold quarries.

By the time the quarrying ended, which was not so many years ago, there were miles of underground workings, some of which had been taken over by the Ministry of Defence during the 1939–45 War. Later a complete underground Whitehall was constructed. Known as **Burlington**, this underground complex included all the departments of state and even a pub. It is also rumoured to have had accommodation for the Royal family. Burlington was constructed during the Cold War and is said to have been radiation proof, the plan being to evacuate the government in the event that nuclear war seemed likely. Exactly whom the underground government was supposed to govern, given the likely death toll of nuclear war and its aftermath, or exactly how they were going to do the governing, is unclear. Although the locals knew of the complex – many were involved in the building works – the general public was not aware of it until Channel 4 broadcast a programme on Burlington. The exact nature of the complex today is still shrouded in mystery.

Almost any walk in the centre of Corsham is worthwhile, such is the wealth of Georgian houses, all in warm Bath stone, and older cottages from the wool trade. It is easy to see why Corsham enchanted Charles Dickens, whose novel *The Pickwick Papers* was inspired by the town. The name may have come from Pickwick Farm, close to the town, although there is also said to have been a local landlord called Moses Pickwick.

When exploring the town, be sure to look for the imposing **church**, the **weavers' cottages** in High Street, and, especially, the **Hungerford Almshouses and Schoolhouse** in Pound Pill. They were built in the 1660s by Lady Margaret Hungerford, who lived at Corsham Court, and are claimed to be one of the finest examples of their style in the country, particularly as they remain virtually as built (though recently restored). There are six almshouses, for town poor, while the schoolhouse – comprising schoolroom and master's house – was for ten poor children. The schoolroom is complete with original desks – and graffiti.

The almshouses are linked by a footpath to **Corsham Court**. The original court was built in 1582. After Paul Methuen, a wealthy wool trader, acquired it in 1745, the north side was remodelled by John Nash in 1800. Half a century later there was further remodelling. The grounds were also landscaped, by both Capability Brown and Humphry Repton. Today, as well as the parkland and house, the Court houses the **Methuen Art Collection**, one of the finest private collections in Britain, which includes works by Van Dyck, Rubens and Reynolds. There is also a comparably fine collection of furniture, with pieces by Adam and Chippendale.

South-west of Corsham is **Box**, famous for Brunel's railway tunnel (see feature box). The village is beautifully set in the steep By Brook valley. A short distance south-east at **Chapel Plaister**, the chapel of the name and the adjacent hospice were built in the 15th century for pilgrims to Glastonbury.

South of Box there are several very neat villages, three of which include fine **Manor Houses**. That at **Monkton Farleigh** was originally a Cluniac priory founded in 1125. At **South Wraxall** the house is a pleasing mix of 15th-century, Elizabethan and Jacobean features. Best of all is **Great Chalfield Manor**, a beautiful mid-15th-century building within a moat and defensive wall. Sadly, the first two buildings are not open to the public, but Great Chalfield Manor is. Now owned by the National Trust, both the house and gardens can be enjoyed. The house, with its Great Hall and exquisite oriel windows, is superb, while the gardens, particularly the rose garden, are equally fine.

South again is **Bradford-on-Avon**, a pretty town, with several outstanding historical features. The town clusters around the River Avon, a web of steep streets filled with a mix of domestic and industrial buildings. Elsewhere such a mix might jar, but here it produces a remarkable harmony, a harmony enhanced by the use of Bath stone. The name is Saxon, from 'broad ford', a crossing of the River Avon, though there was certainly an Iron Age settlement at this strategic point on the river many centuries earlier. The Saxon legacy is **St Lawrence Church**, one of the best survivals in Britain.

The church is a highlight of a short walk which visits the best of the town, but to get the best from a visit a wander through the maze of tight streets should also be made. The walk starts at the **Information Centre** at the centre of the town. Beside it is **Westbury House**, built in the early 18th century by Richard Bethel, a leading clothier when the town was a prosperous wool centre. Originally there was a factory attached to the house. A later owner of both house and factory, Joseph Phelps, installed machinery in the factory, a move which was seen as threatening the livelihood of the town weavers. They marched in protest, the protest soon getting out of hand. A machine was destroyed as protest turned to riot and Phelps shot three of the crowd dead. In the aftermath of the riot and killings the court decided that Phelps' action had been justified and he was awarded compensation for the loss of his machine. Across the street from the house is **'Millie'**, a bronze mill girl erected as part of the millennium celebrations. Millie holds a distaff and spindle, symbolising the wool trade, and, ironically in view of the statue's position, is releasing a dove of peace. Now follow St Margaret's Street towards the Avon bridge. To the right, in Bridge Street, the **town museum** explores Bradford's history. Continue by crossing the bridge, two arches of which date from the 13th century. The lock-up at the near end was added in the 17th century. It was thought it was

Box Tunnel

The Box Tunnel was driven by Isambard Kingdom Brunel (1806–59) to take his railway through Box Hill. At 3,212 yards (2,937m), the tunnel was the longest railway tunnel in Europe for many years. It was built between 1836 and 1841, construction taking about a ton of gunpowder each week. Sadly it also cost the lives of 100 men. The tunnel is absolutely straight and descends on a gradient of 1 in 100 to the east. It is claimed that it was orientated such that the rising sun shines through it on Brunel's birthday (9 April), though there are many who suggest that this story is apocryphal.

originally a toll house, but soon became the place where unruly drunks would spend the night.

Across the bridge the walk bears left into Market Street. Our route turns left into Church Street, but first continue a short distance to see **The Shambles**, to the right, a delightful narrow street of 14th-century houses, though the facades of most are later, probably 17th century. Now follow Church Street to reach the Saxon **St Laurence's church**, on the right. The church was probably built by St Aldhelm of Malmesbury Abbey and so dates from the late 7th/early 8th centuries. It is very rare in being not only extremely old, but for being all of one period, the likely explanation being that when the Normans arrived they built their own church rather than extending the existing one, perhaps because it was too small. St Laurence's then became redundant and was later converted into a house and, later, a schoolroom. Only in the 1870s was it realised that beneath the 'modern' building there was such a rarity. The church is open to visitors daily.

Further along, on the left, is **Holy Trinity Church**, the Norman building which replaced St Laurence's. It was begun in the 12th century, but has been modified since. At the end of the street a path to the right reaches Newtown. Bear left, then right to reach a path which passes **St Mary's Tory**, a chapel built in the 16th century at what was then the highest point of the town. Further on are a series of weavers' cottages. To the modern eye these are charming, but at the height of the wool trade they were considered much less attractive, being small and poorly sited.

To continue, return to the path followed from Church Street, but now bear right to walk downhill, soon reaching the 14th-century **packhorse bridge** which spans the Avon. Cross to reach **Barton Grange Farm**. The enormous tithe barn here dates from the early 14th century. The barn was owned by Shaftesbury Abbey and would have been filled with the tithes from farmers working Abbey lands. They contributed a tenth (hence 'tithe') of their produce, the barn's size an indication both of the fertility of local land and the wealth of the Abbey. The Barton Farm complex also has a granary and manor house from the same period as the tithe barn.

Close to Bradford, **Westwood Manor House** was described by Pevsner as 'a perfect Wilshire manor house'. It was originally built in about 1400, but there have been additions over the centuries since then, all beautifully matched to maintain the harmony of the building. Inside there is a wealth of period furniture, some fine tapestries and a collection of stringed instruments. The gardens include good topiary. A short distance to the west, the **Peto Garden** at **Iford Manor** is the work of Harold Peto (1854–1933) who, in partnership with Ernest George, created an Italian-style garden of great beauty and interest. The garden, much more formal than the usual English form, is enhanced by Renaissance architecture and statuary. The Manor itself also has Italianesque touches, with the cloisters, which were built only in 1913, now being used for an annual series of opera productions.

Bath

Although it is over the border in Somerset, few visitors will get this close to Bath and not want to see England's finest Georgian city. Below a short history of the city is given, together with details of the major visitor attractions it offers.

Bath's origins are steeped in mystery. It is likely that earliest man knew of the existence of the hot springs, although as the surrounding area is likely to have been a salt marsh, he may not have had a home here. According to legend the town was built by Prince Bladud, a descendant of refugees from Troy, and father of Shakespeare's King Lear. The poor prince contracted leprosy and was immediately banished from court to live out his days as a pig herder in the marshes. Inevitably one of the pigs also contracted leprosy, but to Bladud's astonishment it was cured after taking a mud-bath near the hot springs. Bladud then tried the mud-bath himself and he, too, was cured, and allowed back to court. To commemorate this legendary founding of the city, about 2,800 years ago, there is a statue of Bladud at the Cross Bath.

The archaeological evidence of the founding of the city is more mundane. It is likely that the first town was Roman, *Aquæ Sulis* – the waters of the goddess Sulis – constructed in the first century AD. The Romans were undoubtedly tempted by the million or so litres (250,000 gallons) of water at 50°C (120°F) that rushes to the surface daily, and constructed a town around the public baths. The baths themselves are a minor wonder, with central heating in all rooms, a sauna and, of course, the pool, all fed by the hot waters.

When the Romans left, the town quickly decayed. The Saxon invaders, reaching here after the battle at Dyrham, to the north, could only wonder at the building. They were not great builders themselves and they believed the town was the work of giants, and haunted. Certainly the decaying buildings and the deep, warm pools, all overgrown, must have been ghostly. Gradually the site became holy, probably fired by superstition and legend, and King Offa founded an abbey here. This became an important site, and King Edgar was crowned here, the first king of all Saxon England, in 973. The abbot and the townspeople of medieval Bath knew of the hot waters and their medicinal purposes, for there are early

references to people visiting the town to bathe in the waters. Indeed the visitors were a major source of income to the townspeople.

The bathers were subject to no regulations, however, and the baths became so unwholesome that people were reluctant to use them. In 1533 the chief bathers were those with 'lepre, pokkes, scabbes and great aches' and since there was no filtration or changing of the water it is hardly surprising that the baths were described as stinking. Bath had to wait 200 years for the coming of a gentler age, when **Richard (Beau) Nash** regulated the bathing, stopped the sedan chair carriers from overcharging, erected theatres, assembly rooms and houses, and controlled the gambling that was at the heart of Bath's social position. The whole Georgian city is really a tribute to the energy of this one man, who died in 1761 at the great age of 88. His statue stands in the Pump Room, which dispenses warm salty water freely to visitors.

Walking Tour

Bath Abbey is a masterpiece: it was started about 1500 on the site of an older, Norman, church following a dream by Oliver King, Bishop of Bath and Wells, in which he saw angels climbing ladders to heaven and was told to rebuild the older church. The abbey's west front follows King's dream with angels climbing ladders on either side.

The architects employed by King promised him that 'ther shal be noone so goodly in england nor in fraunce'. And who would argue with the truth of that promise? A statue of Bishop King can be seen inside.

The walls inside the abbey are covered with numerous memorials to the rich who retired to Bath to take the waters in an attempt to improve their failing health. There is also a memorial to Beau Nash. Prior Birde's notable **chantry** is on the south side of the chancel. The stonework here is magnificent – so much so that the time spent by the masons on its construction bankrupted the benefactor. The **Abbey Heritage Vaults** house a collection of items illustrating the site's history.

In the courtyard (known as Abbey Churchyard) in front of the abbey are the **Pump Room** (built at the latter end of the 18th century) and the **Roman Baths**. The Roman Museum at the Pump Room houses many of the items found during excavations on the site and elsewhere in the city. Particularly notable is the fierce head of Medusa, a stone carving from the Roman Temple. West of here are two of the original baths, the **Cross Bath** in Bath Street and, to the left, the **Hot Bath**.

Bear right at the Hot Bath to reach Westgate Buildings, turning right there to reach the **Theatre Royal**, part of which was once Beau Nash's house. Close by is the house of Nash's last mistress, Juliana Popjoy.

William Herschel, an organist, lived in New King Street, to the west of the theatre: he made telescopes as a hobby and used one to discover the planet Uranus, later becoming Astronomer Royal. His house in New King Street – at No. 19 – is now a **museum** of his music and astronomy.

Continue north, soon reaching

Queen Square. This is considered to be one of the best works in the city by John Wood the Elder, who with his son, John the Younger, formed the principal team of architects of the Georgian city that lies to the north of the baths. The **obelisk** is, again, a commemoration by Beau Nash, this time of Frederick, Prince of Wales.

Running north from the Square is **Gay Street**, built by the Woods; Josiah Wedgwood, the famous pottery manufacturer, lived here at No. 30. Turn left along Queen's Parade. Here there are the last remaining examples in Britain of sedan chair houses, two small gate houses where chair carriers would wait for passengers. Just beyond, turn right along Gravel Walk, soon passing the **Georgian Garden**. The garden is a recreation of the original one of 1760, using an excavated plan and authentic plant species. It was in this garden, in Jane Austen's *Persuasion*, that Captain Wentworth and Anne Elliot declared their love. At 40 Gay Street the **Jane Austen Centre** is a celebration of Bath's association with the writer.

Gravel Walk leads into Royal Victoria Park, which fronts **Royal Crescent**, perhaps the best known and loved of all Bath's buildings. The Crescent is by John Wood the Younger, and is superbly set off by the lawns and trees in front of it. Sir Isaac Pitman lived here, and from here Sheridan eloped with Elizabeth Linley. **No. 1 Royal Crescent** is owned by the Bath Preservation Trust, and has been completely restored to show how an elegant Bath town house would have looked in the 18th century.

From Royal Crescent, go eastwards

Above: Tithe barn, Bradford-on-Avon
Below: The Royal Crescent, Bath
Opposite page: Bath Abbey from the Roman Baths

along Brock Street to **The Circus**, a magnificent circular street lined with fine buildings by the Woods. Here lived, though not at the same time, William Pitt, Thomas Gainsborough and David Livingstone. Just off the Circus, in Bennett Street, the **Museum of East Asian Art** has a collection of art from China, Japan, Korea, Thailand and Indonesia.

Continue east along Bennett Street, turning first right to reach the **Assembly Rooms**, by Wood the Younger. At the Assembly Rooms is the **Museum of Costume**, one of the world's largest displays, covering fashion back to medieval times, and including exhibitions of jewellery. An extension of the museum that holds the library of books, magazines and photographs of fashion, is at No. 4 The Circus.

Turn left along Alfred Street, then first right down Bartlett Street, soon reaching George Street. A left turn here, then another and a right at the fork leads to the **Building of Bath Museum**, which deals with the architectural history of the city.

Our walk turns right along George Street, then left down Milsom Street, one of the city's main shopping streets. Soon a left turn into **Shire's Yard** visits not only a delightful shopping square (and one of Bath's best coffee houses), but allows a short cut to Broad Street and the **Postal Museum**. Bath has very strong links with the postal service, and is grateful to it. Ralph Allen, a Cornishman, rented the postal service from the Government in the late 17th century and made it efficient and profitable. In the process he became rich, and his arrival in Bath, around 1710, was the start of Bath's

rise to fame. It was Allen who saw the potential of the hot springs and bought the Combe Down quarries that supplied the stone for his architect, John Wood the Elder, who designed Allen's own house, near the abbey. All aspects of the postal service and the Royal Mail are covered in the museum.

Bear left along New Bond Street, then turn right into Northgate Street. Ahead is High Street and the **Guildhall**, a fine Georgian building of 1776 with what is widely regarded as the finest Adam-style interior in Britain. The Banqueting Room on the first floor is magnificent. It is lit by a crystal chandelier of 1778 and hung with portraits of some of the famous people associated with Bath. Turn left into Bridge Street. To the right at the end the **Victoria Art Gallery** houses, in addition to paintings, fine collections of glass and ceramics, and items of local interest. Many times during the year there are special exhibitions covering a range of subjects.

Bridge Street leads to **Pulteney Bridge**, built in 1769 by Robert Adam. It is one of the few bridges with shops now surviving in Europe. At the far end of Great Pulteney Street, beyond the bridge is the **Holburne Museum of Art**. This houses the collections of Sir William Holburne: paintings, including works by Gainsborough, Stubbs and Turner; silver, one of the finest collections in Britain; porcelain and glass; bronzes and enamels. In addition to the set collections, there are special exhibitions during the year, and a Craft Study Centre for modern craftwork in metal and glass. Outside, the gardens are also of interest.

Turn right along Grand Parade. Bear right here, crossing to **Orange Grove**, named after the Prince of Orange. At its centre is an obelisk raised by Beau Nash to commemorate the Prince's visit to the city. Do not follow the Grove, which leads back to the Abbey, but continue south, bearing right along Terrace Walk and turning right into North Parade Passage. Here, and in nearby Old Lilliput Alley, are some of Bath's oldest houses, built around 1500. **Sally Lunn's**, named after a Georgian pastrycook, is claimed to be the oldest. It has a restored Georgian kitchen and is an excellent coffee house, selling Sally Lunn's Buns, perhaps not as famous as Bath buns, but just as delicious.

Other Places of Interest

Away from the city centre there are three further museums. The **Museum of Bath at Work** is at the Camden Works, Julian Street, to the north of the Assembly Rooms: here the visitor can get away from the social elegance of Georgian Bath to discover how the ordinary city dweller lived in the 18th and 19th centuries. The works themselves are an exact reconstruction of a Victorian brass foundry and a Bath stone quarry face, with other exhibits illustrating different industries and lifestyles. Children will love the old plant for putting fizz in fizzy drinks; the drinks are on sale.

About half a mile (1km) north-east of the abbey, on the southern bank of the Avon, in Forester Road is the **Bath Boathouse**, a near-perfect Victorian boathouse where punts can still be hired. For the less skilled there are also skiffs.

The **American Museum** at Claverton Manor, 2 miles (3km) east of the city centre, shows the history of North America from the time of the Pilgrim Fathers, with period rooms containing fine examples of American furniture: exhibits deal with the opening of the West and with the Indians, and in the gardens there are several exhibits including a covered wagon. The gardens of the manor are also worth visiting.

Also near Claverton, the **Pumping Station** of the Kennet and Avon Canal used a 16ft (5m) waterwheel to drive a pump which lifted water from the River Avon into the canal. The waterwheel was driven by the river. Now restored, the pump operates on certain summer days, but can be seen throughout the summer.

A bus or taxi is needed to reach the National Trust's **Prior Park** as there is only limited disabled parking at the site. The 18th-century garden was landscaped by Capability Brown for Ralph Allen and has typical follies and a lake. The Park has been carefully restored and includes several miles of woodland walking. The views of Bath from the Park are breathtaking.

Finally – and there is a great temptation to say 'at last' because of the delays – the new **Thermae Bath Spa** has opened. Years in the doing, and millions in the costing, the new centre has four bathing pools, including a rooftop pool, together with steam rooms and treatment rooms, all using the city's thermal waters. There is also a restaurant and Visitor Centre.

Places to Visit

Chippenham

Museum and Heritage Centre

10 Market Place
Open: All year, Mon–Sat 10am–4pm.
Open on Bank Holidays except at
Christmas.
☎ 01249 705020

Wiltshire and Swindon History Centre

Cocklebury Road
Open: All year Tue–Sat 9.30am–
5.30pm. Closed on Bank Holidays.
☎ 01249 705500

Sheldon Manor

Open: Only on days related to
National Gardens scheme. Also
open to groups.
☎ 01249 653120

Lackham Museum of Agriculture and Rural Life

Open: Aug, daily 10am–5pm. Also at
other times for special events.
☎ 01249 466847/466800

Lacock Abbey (National Trust)

Lacock
Open: Abbey, Apr–Oct, daily
except Tue and Good Fri 1–5pm.
Abbey Cloisters and Grounds, Mar–
Oct, daily except Good Fri 11am–
5pm. Fox Talbot Museum, open as
the Cloisters and Grounds, and also
Nov–Feb Sat and Sun 11am–4pm.
Closed Christmas and New Year.
☎ 01249 730459

Calne

Bowood House and Gardens

Open: Sat closest to 1 Apr–Oct,
daily 11am–6pm (House closes at
5.30pm).
☎ 01249 812102

Calne Heritage Centre

New Road
Open: All year, Wed–Sat 10am–4pm,
Sun 1–5pm.
☎ 01249 820066

Atwell-Wilson Motor Museum

Downside, Stockley Lane
Open: Apr–Oct, daily except Fri
11am–5pm. Nov–Mar daily except
Fri and Sat 11am–4pm. Also open
on Good Fri.
☎ 01249 813119.

Devizes

Wadworth Brewery

Northgate Brewery
Open: Reception Centre: all year,
Mon–Fri 8.30am–5pm. Closed on
Bank Holidays. Shire Horse Stables:
all year, Mon–Thu 1.30–3.30pm.
Closed on Bank Holidays. Groups of
more than 6 people must pre-book.
☎ 01380 723361

Kennet and Avon Canal Trust Museum

Couch Lane
Open: Mar–Christmas, daily 10am–
4pm.
☎ 01380 721279

Wiltshire Heritage

41 Long Street
Open: All year, Tue–Fri 10am–5pm.
Closed on Bank Holidays, but open on occasional Sats.
☎ 01380 727369

Broadleas Gardens

Broadleas
Open: Mar–Oct, Sun, Wed and Thu 2–6pm.
☎ 01380 722035

Corsham

Lady Hungerford Almshouses and Schoolhouse

Pound Pill
Open: Easter–Sep, Tue, Wed, Fri and Sat 1.30–4pm. Oct, Nov, Feb and Mar, Sat 1–3pm.
☎ 01249 701414 (during opening hours only). At other times ask at the Tourist Information Office.

Corsham Court

Open: mid-Mar–Sep, daily except Mon and Fri (but open on Bank Holidays) 2–5.30pm. Oct–mid-Mar (but closed throughout Dec) Sat and Sun 2–4.30pm.
☎ 01249 701610.

Bradford-on-Avon

Town Museum

Bridge Street
Open: Easter–Oct, Mon–Sat 10.30am–12.30pm and 2–4pm. Sun and Bank Holidays 2–4pm.
Nov–Easter (but closed mid-Dec to mid-Jan) Wed–Fri and Sun 2–4pm, Sat 10.30am–12.30pm and 2–4pm.
☎ 01225 863280 or 868127

Barton Farm (English Heritage)

Open: All year, daily 10.30am–4pm.
Closed on Christmas Day.
No telephone.

Great Chalfield Manor (National Trust)

Open: House: Apr–Oct, Tue, Wed and Thu, Guided tours at 11.30am, 12.15pm, 2.15pm and 3.45pm. Sun, Guided tours at 2.15pm, 3pm and 3.45pm.
☎ 01225 782239

Corsham Court

Places to Visit

Westwood Manor House
(National Trust)

Westwood
Open: mid-Mar–Sep, Tue, Wed and
Sun 2–5pm.
☎ 01225 863374

Iford Manor
(The Peto Garden)

Open: May–Sep, daily except Mon
and Fri 2–5pm. Apr and Oct, Sun
2–5pm.
☎ 01225 863146

Bath

American Museum

Claverton Manor, Claverton
Open: mid-Mar–Oct, daily (except
Mon) 12noon–5pm.
☎ 01225 460503

Assembly Rooms and
Costume Museum

Bennett Street
Open: All year daily 11am–5pm (4pm
in Jan, Feb, Nov and Dec).
☎ 01225 477173

Bath Abbey

Open: Easter–Novr, Mon–Sat
9am–6pm, Sun 1.30–2.30pm and
4.30–5.30pm. Nov–Easter, Mon–Sat
9am–4.30pm, Sun 1.30–2.30pm and
4.30–5.30pm. The Heritage Vaults
(☎ 01225 422462) are open all year
Mon–Sat 10am–4pm.
☎ 01225 422462

Bath Boathouse

Forester Road
Open: Apr–Sep, daily 10am–6pm.
☎ 01225 466407

Building of Bath Museum

Huntingdon's Chapel, The Vineyards,
The Paragon
Open: Mid-Feb–Nov Tue–Sun and
Bank Holiday Mon 10.30am–5pm.
☎ 01225 333895

Claverton Pumping Station

Ferry Lane, Claverton
Open: Easter–late Oct, Sun and Bank
Holidays 10am–5pm. Pumping on
certain days only.
☎ 0117 986 7536

Georgian Garden

Gravel Walk
Open: May–Oct, daily 9am–7pm
☎ 01225 477752

Guildhall

High Street
Open: All year, Mon–Fri 9am–5pm
unless being used for a special
function.
☎ 01225 477724

Holburne Museum of Art

Great Pulteney Street
Open: All year Tue–Sat 10am–5pm,
Bank Holiday Mon and Sun 11am–
5pm.
☎ 01225 466669

Jane Austen Centre

40 Gay Street
Open: All year daily 10am–5.30pm

(4.30pm Nov–Feb).
☎ 01225 443000

Museum of Bath at Work

Camden Works, Julian Road
Open: Easter to Oct, daily 10am–5pm; Nov to Easter, Sat and Sun 10am–5pm.
☎ 01225 318348

Museum of East Asian Art

12 Bennett Street
Open: All year Tue–Sat 10am–5pm, Sun 12noon–5pm.
☎ 01225 464640

No. 1 Royal Crescent

Open: Mid-Feb–Oct, Tue–Sun and Bank Holiday and Bath Festival Mons 10.30am–5pm; Nov, Tue–Sun 10.30am–4pm.
☎ 01225 428126

Postal Museum

8 Broad Street
Open: all year, Mon–Sat 11am–5pm.
☎ 01225 460333

Prior Park (National Trust)

Ralph Allen Drive
Open: all year daily except Tue 12noon–5.30 or dusk.
Disabled visitors should ring to reserve one of the three disabled parking bays. There is no parking for other visitors, who must arrive by bus or taxi.
☎ 0225 833422

Roman Baths and Museum

Pump Room
Open: Mar–Oct daily 9am–6pm (9pm in Jul and Aug), Dec–Feb daily 9.30am–5.30pm. Closed 25 and 26 Dec. Last entry 1 hour before closing.
☎ 01225 477785

Sally Lunn's

4 North Parade Passage
Open: all year. Museum: Mon–Sat 10am–6pm, Sun 12noon–6pm. Teashop: Mon–Sat 10am–11pm, Sun 12noon–11pm.
☎ 01225 461634

Thermae Bath Spa

The Hetling Pump Room, Hot Bath Street
Open: Daily (except Christmas Day, New Year's Eve and New Year's Day) 9am–10pm. Last entry 8pm.
☎ 01225 331234

Victoria Art Gallery

Bridge Street
Open: all year, Tue–Fri 10am–5.30pm, Sat 10am–5pm. Closed Bank Holidays.
☎ 01225 477233

William Herschel Museum

19 New King Street
Open: Feb–mid-Dec, daily 1–5pm.
☎ 01225 446865

3. East Wiltshire: The Ridgeway

The east of the county is dominated by high downland. On its crest is the Ridgeway claimed by some to be the oldest road in Europe. At its western foot lies Avebury, which many suggest is an even more significant prehistoric site than Stonehenge, and several other marvellous ancient places. Here too are Marlborough, a lovely old town, Savernake Forest and a museum which explores the bygone age of canals.

South of Swindon, beyond the M4 lies a wide ridge of chalk downland, a continuation of the Salisbury Plain. The ridge is followed by the **Ridgeway**, a National Trail (i.e. a waymarked – with the acorn symbol of all such trails – and maintained long-distance footpath). The Trail is relatively new, but the route it follows is an ancient one for it is believed that men have used the downland as a trade or migration route since before recorded history. To see the best scenery and to visit the most historic sites, it is best to follow the Trail, but here we visit accessible sites along it, starting with the ancient site that is, in many ways, more important (though less spectacular) than Stonehenge itself.

Avebury

Most visitors come to **Avebury** to see the great megalithic site, but the village is also worth visiting. The main village car park lies to the south and is linked by a path to the High Street where the National Trust, which owns the Avebury site, the stone avenue and other local parcels of land, as well as the Great Barn complex, has a shop. The **Great Barn**, once known as the Parson's Barn, is a magnificent 17th-century thatched tithe barn and is now the centrepiece of a rural life exhibition exploring Wiltshire life in the late 19th and early 20th centuries.

Close to the Great Barn is **St James' Church**. The first church on the site was Saxon and parts of this still remain (three small round windows on the north nave wall), but this was incorporated into a Norman building which was expanded several times. The font is Saxon, but the plain Saxon cylinder was decorated with carvings in early Norman times. Across from the church is the **Alexander Keiller Museum**, which houses the best finds excavated from Windmill Hill and the other local sites. The finds are one of the best Neolithic collections in Britain.

Just beyond the museum is **Avebury Manor**, built on the site of the Benedictine Priory founded in the 12th century. The museum is actually housed in the coach house and stables of the manor, which was begun in the mid-16th century, using stone from the priory and from the breaking up of standing stones from the megalithic sites. In the 1930s Alexander Keiller, the leader of the team of excavators on Windmill Hill and the man responsible for re-erecting some of the Avebury stones, bought the manor, making it the centre of his Morven Institute for archaeological research. It is known that John Aubrey and William Stukeley – two antiquarians linked to excavations of local prehistoric sites – both stayed at the house, so it has a proud place in the history of the unravelling of Avebury's secrets. When Keiller sold his Avebury lands in 1942 the National Trust could not afford the manor, which remained in private hands until the Trust finally acquired it in the late 1980s.

One final point of interest is the **Tourist Information Centre**, which is located within a 17th-century Nonconformist chapel. The chapel is believed to be the only one to be sited within a stone circle, while the centre is believed to be the only one within a working chapel.

In 1663 King Charles II was travelling to Bath with the antiquarian John Aubrey and the two decided to make a short detour to see the **Megalithic Site** which, even then, was famous. Aubrey was impressed. 'It does as much exceed in greatness the so renowned Stonehenge', he wrote 'as a cathedral doth a parish church.' For many visitors the initial reaction is that Avebury is less impressive than Stonehenge, but after a walk around and a contemplation of its complexity and size, many reconsider and agree with Aubrey. When complete the main Avebury monument covered over 28 acres (11 hectares), and was circled by a ditch 1,500 yards (1,350m) long – it is 380 yards (350m) in diameter – that was up to 30 feet (9m) deep and a bank nearly 20 feet (almost 7m) high. Inside were around 250 standing stones, the tallest nearly 25 feet (over 7m) high, some weighing over 60 tons. This complex was linked by an avenue of 100 pairs of standing stones to **The Sanctuary** 1¼ miles (almost 2km) away and (probably) to another avenue heading towards Beckhampton. The sheer engineering effort is breathtaking and is estimated to have taken over 1½ million man-hours, at a time when the local population was probably numbered in thousands.

As with Stonehenge, Avebury was not constructed in one vast effort. It is believed that the outer ditch was dug in about 2700BC, after the first phase of The Sanctuary (and also the completion of the first phase of Stonehenge) and completed by about 2300BC, perhaps 200 years before Stonehenge's final phases. When completed the site comprised a roughly circular ditch/bank – the actual shape is sufficiently irregular to suggest that for all their undoubted engineering sophistication the builders did not have very accurate surveying methods and that the construction was piecemeal, with gangs of diggers working towards each other and sometimes not meeting as they might have hoped – pierced by four entranceways. These entrances now carry the main road and Avebury High Street. Just within the ditch was a circle of standing stones formed of 98 stones, of which only 30 remain (three of which have fallen and not been re-erected). Within this circle there were two further stone circles, each of which had a further feature at its centre. These two smaller circles have few of the 30 or so stones they originally comprised. At the centre of the northern circle is a collection of three upright stones, forming a row which appears to be aligned to the moon's most northerly point of rising. At the centre of the southern circle is a more complex arrangement of stones.

A walk around the outer stone circle is very worthwhile, just to gauge the size of the site and the stones. The so-called **Portal Stones** (Stones 1 and 98, to the right of the road as you reach the site from The Sanctuary) are each 14 feet (4m) high and must have formed an impressive entranceway. At the opposite side of the circle, Stone 46 (called the **Swindon Stone** as it lies beside the

Destroying the Stones

The absence of many of the stones from the Avebury site is due, in large part, to their destruction in medieval times. William Stukeley records that periodically pits were dug beneath the stones and filled with straw which was then set alight. The heated stone was then doused with cold water, after which it could be easily broken up with hammers. This has often been portrayed as a Christian ritual, the church supervising the symbolic destruction of a pagan emblem. In fact it was merely the easy production of building stone for the expanding village of Avebury. The legend of a church ritual probably derives from the discovery that many of the stones had been dropped and buried in earlier times in what was certainly an attempt to deprive the site of its power.

That so many stones survive is due to this earlier burying and the efforts of Alexander Keiller – heir to a marmalade 'empire' and an amateur (but very good) archaeologist – who bought the site in 1930 and re-erected the excavated stones. During the raising of Stone 9 (the 6th stone from either end of the south-west sector of the outer stone circle) the remains of a man were found. Coins found on the man dated his death to about 1320 and it is assumed that he was part of a team dropping and burying the stone and was crushed when it fell. No attempt had been made to extract his body for burial. Other finds on the skeletal remains suggest the man was an itinerant barber-surgeon: perhaps he was in Avebury for just a day or two, and joined in for the fun of it – fun until the stone fell, that is.

road to Swindon) is estimated to be the site's heaviest at about 65 tons.

William Stukeley drew a map of Avebury and the nearby sites in 1743 showing two avenues, one leading to The Sanctuary, the other towards Beckhampton. Stukeley contrived to make the combination look like a snake: he also 'adjusted' his measurements and stone positions to fit his own view of the sites, which he believed were Druidic in origins. The **West Kennet Avenue**, leading to The Sanctuary, is clearly visible, though the Beckhampton avenue is more speculative. The West Kennet Avenue comprised about 100 pairs of stones. These, as with the main Avebury sites, but unlike Stonehenge, were not dressed, but erected as found. Some experts have seen a regular pattern of triangular and phallic shapes in the stones and gone on to speculate a fertility rite basis for the avenue's existence: others are less convinced.

South of Avebury

To the south of Avebury, lying beside the A4 to the west of West Kennet is **Silbury Hill**, perhaps the most enigmatic of the ancient sites. The hill is the largest man-made mound in Europe – as large as the smaller of Egypt's great pyramids. A tunnel dug into the centre of the hill has revealed that the mound was constructed in three phases, the first in about 2700BC, the last about 400 years later. It is ironic that science can tell us that the first phase – the building of a mound about 120 feet (36m) in diameter, 15 feet (4½m) high – started in late summer (probably August) because winged ants were trapped in the cut turfs, but can tell us nothing about why it was built. The second mound was conical, but the final mound was similar to the step pyramid, with circular retaining walls rising from flat shelves. The shelves were then infilled with soil to create a smooth cone with a face angle of 60 degrees, though the top was left flat. The mound is 130 feet (40m) high and 175 yards (160m) in diameter. It covers five acres (2 hectares) and required the moving of about 14 million cubic feet

West Kennet Long Barrow interior

King Sel and Silbury

One local legend states that the Silbury Hill mound is the tomb of an as yet undiscovered king, King Sel. The legend maintains that the king was buried upright with his horse and that both wear armour of solid gold.

(400,000 cubic metres) of chalk.

Given the statistics the mound was clearly very important – so what was it for? It lies in a valley and is not easily seen from a distance, so it was obviously not meant to make an impression on arriving travellers. It was not visible from the Avebury site when the banks were at full height. Excavations have revealed no burials, either of men, animals or treasure, so it does not appear to have been a vast tomb. Despite endless speculation, there are no firm conclusions regarding the hill's purpose. Please note that the mound may not be climbed.

Close to Silbury Hill – go east along the A4 for a short distance to reach a signed path on the right – the **West Kennet Long Barrow** is one of the best-preserved Neolithic tombs in Britain. It is also one of the most impressive, its entranceway closed by vast 'blocking' stones. Beyond these – it is possible to edge between them – a passageway with two pairs of side burial chambers finishes at a fifth chamber. The passage and chambers are roofed with large flat slabs and the whole covered with a huge earth mound. This mound is 110 yards (100m) long, second in length of British barrows only to that at East Kennet. Of this length,

East Wiltshire: The Ridgeway

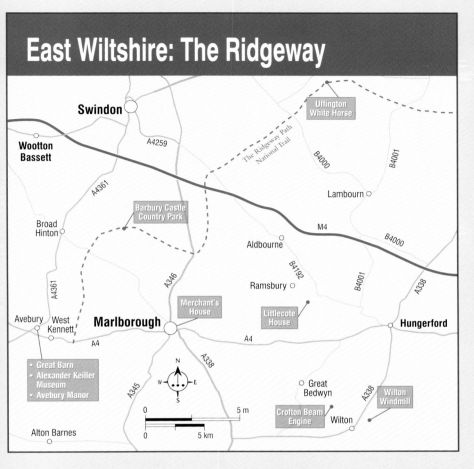

only about 40 feet (12m) is taken up by the burial passage: the rest appears to be earth alone.

It is thought the tomb was constructed around 3500BC, but continued in use for around 1,500 years, the final sealing with the blocking stone slabs being in about 2000BC. Excavations revealed skeletal fragments of 46 bodies, not many for so long a use, but the way the bones were piled up and the fact that few skeletons were complete implies that periodic clearing or sorting of the bones may have taken place. When constructed, the barrow had a ditch running along each side and a forecourt in front of the entrance, presumably for rituals associated with new burials. The elaborate facade of the barrow is its most impressive feature, and was presumably of great symbolic importance, so much so that it comprises not only local sarsen stones, but slabs of oolitic limestone brought to the site from the Bath area.

Further east along the A4, the visitor can turn right for **East Kennet**, a neat village, notable for its little church and for the tree-clad **long barrow** set on the overshadowing down. The long barrow is the longest in Britain, 16 feet (5m) longer than West Kennet, but has never been excavated. Such burial chambers and objects as it does contain may have been damaged by the roots of the trees that now shroud it. **West Overton**, the next village, has a 16th-century manor house beside the church.

On the main road is **Fyfield**, famous for the down to the north which bears its name. **Fyfield Down** is littered with sarsen stones and is believed to be the source of the stones for the Avebury complex and Stonehenge. As well as being a 'quarry' for the megalithic builders, Fyfield also has its own sites, one of which is known as the **Devil's Den**. This is a dolmen or cromlech, a Neolithic long barrow from which the overtopping earth mound – the barrow – has eroded. The Down also shows evidence of post-megalithic use, Iron Age (Celtic) and Roman field systems

being present and a Saxon track (Herapath or Green Street) running along the northern edge of these systems. The name 'herapath' is interesting – it means 'army track': this is the way the Saxons came on their westward push.

South of East Kennet is **Alton Barnes**, where the church is Saxon, but with a 15th-century wooden roof. The church lies just a stone's throw from the more substantial church in the neighbouring hamlet of **Alton Priors**. Beside the road to the Alton villages is a **white horse** cut in 1812 by Robert Pile, a local farmer. It is the biggest of all the Wiltshire horses, filling a 165ft (50m) square. Legend has it that Pile gave John Thorne, a local painter, £20 to design and cut the horse. Thorne produced a sketch, persuaded another man to start work and promptly disappeared with the £20. Pile was forced to finish the work himself; later Thorne was hanged, though it is not clear if this

---

Sarsen Stones

The chalk of the Wiltshire and Berkshire Downs was laid down beneath a calm sea – chalk being no more than a very fine-grained, soft limestone – during the Cretaceous period of geological time. During later eras the chalk was covered with a thin layer of a hard sandstone. Sandstone is, as the name implies, created from sand, a desert then existing where a clear sea had previously washed. Sand is converted into rock by a process known as diagenesis in which some form of cement glues the sand grains together. Subsequent earth movements broke the thin sandstone layer into slabs of various sizes, littering Fyfield Down with blocks of stone. It was these blocks which the megalithic (meaning, literally, 'large stone') builders used to create their monuments. The blocks are known as sarsens, though the origin of the world is not well understood: many believe it derives from 'Saracen' as the monuments were seen as being of pagan (i.e. non-Christian) origin in medieval times. The local name for the blocks is 'grey wethers', meaning grey sheep, as from a distance they are hard to distinguish from grazing sheep.

was simply for his theft of Pile's cash. Closer to the scarp road than the white horse is **Adam's Grave**, a chambered long barrow and the remains of a Neolithic camp.

North of Avebury

North-west of Avebury is the final site of the complex of prehistoric sites around the village. **Windmill Hill** is topped by a causeway camp, a series of three concentric ditches/banks breached by chalk causeways. The outer ditch encloses an area of 21 acres (8.5 hectares), making Windmill Hill one of the largest Neolithic camps discovered to date. The exact purpose of the enclosure is unclear. Similar sites were obviously inhabited by people living in permanent huts, but at Windmill Hill excavations suggest seasonal occupation only, perhaps for feasting as the ditches are full of animal bones and pottery shards. But there are also human bones too, suggesting that the site also had a funereal function. A square enclosure just outside the outer ditch is believed to have been the site of cremations and 'sky' burials and, after the bones had been picked clean, for rituals which culminated in some bones being put into the ditches. Quite why some bones were disposed of with household rubbish and what happened to the bones that were not thrown in the ditches is not known, but most experts now believe the rituals carried out here and at the other local sites involved some form of ancestor worship.

The main road north from Avebury passes through **Winterbourne Monkton**, a pretty village with a church with an unusual shingled belfry. The first part of the name is the old local name for the stream that forms the upper reaches of the Kennet. It was a *winterbourne*, a winter stream, summer's waters often disappearing into the chalk. Further north, a left turn crosses a humpback bridge over the winterbourne to reach **Berwick Bassett**, another pretty village, one with two manor houses, the older 15th century, the other a couple of centuries newer. The next village to the north, which also lies off the main road, is also named for the winter stream. **Winterbourne Bassett** is less pretty than its neighbours, but has a lovely little church: look for the memorials to the Baskerville family and the weathered 13th-century effigy figures.

East of these villages is the **Barbury Castle Country Park**. The castle is an Iron Age hillfort, the natural defences of the downland slopes being reinforced by two rings of ditches and ramparts, these enclosing an area of 11½ acres (4.5 hectares). Unlike Windmill Hill, this hillfort was almost certainly a purely defensive structure, though there is evidence of huts inside, indicating seasonal occupation or, perhaps, a permanent garrison at some stage. Hillforts were not used for permanent occupation, the local population retreating to the fort when an invading enemy threatened. The Country Park encloses the castle and surrounding area, and has a picnic area, toilets and car parks. The hillfort lies on the Ridgeway National Trail (see Factfile at the end of the book).

North-east of Barbury towards the M4, another hillfort, **Liddington Castle**, lies close to, but not on, the Na-

Alton Barnes

tional Trail, and is therefore usually far quieter. North-east of Liddington, visitors reach **Bishopstone**, the last village in Wiltshire before the border with Berkshire is crossed. Few will ignore the chance at this point to travel on a few miles to see the **Uffington white horse**, the most famous and enigmatic of all the horses carved into the chalk of central England's downland.

From Liddington, it is a short distance south-east to **Aldbourne**, a pretty village built around a duckpond, and a green with an old cross. The church, which overlooks the green, is worth visiting to see two late-18th-century fire engines (complete with instructions for use; the pair are known, inevitably, as Adam and Eve) and the carved alabaster tomb of John Stone, an early 16th-century vicar. Anciently Aldbourne was famous for its bell foundry, chiefly making bells for animals rather than churches, and for willow and straw

Obtaining water on Barbury Hill

Iron Age sieges were unlikely to have been very long-lasting because of the difficulties of keeping an army in the field, but on chalk the defenders would have needed to solve the water problem as Barbury, like other local hillforts, is built well above the spring line. The defenders could have brought water in leather buckets, but that would have taken time. It is more likely that they used dew ponds, a method of collecting water that the downland farmers continued to use until electric pumps allowed valley water to be pumped to upland troughs. Dew ponds were large excavated depressions lined with clay to make them waterproof, the clay being mixed with soot which deterred worms and burrowing insects that might have caused leaks. The ponds were filled by rain or condensing clouds.

Barbury Memorial

The Barbury Castle Country Park includes a standing stone memorial to two local writers. **Richard Jefferies** (1848–87) was a reporter on the *North Wilts Herald* who wrote about 20 books on the local way of life and Wiltshire characters. He is now recognised as one of the 19th century's finest writers on pastoral life, and his lyricism can still strike a chord today. Jeffries was born at Coate, then a village to the south-east of Swindon, now one of the town's suburbs. There is a bust to his memory in Salisbury Cathedral. **Alfred Williams** (1877-1930), another local man, was a naturalist and gifted poet. Words from each of these fine writers are inscribed on their memorial tablets.

---

plaiting.

From Aldbourne the B4192, and then a country lane, lead to **Ramsbury**. The church here houses two coped stones from a 9th-century Saxon church on the same site, and several

Aldbourne

very good memorials. Close to the church, **Parliament Piece** is a superb late-17th-century brick house. There are two good inns, the **Malt Shovel** and the **Bell**; in front of the Bell stood the **Ramsbury Elm**, believed to have seeded when Charles I was on the throne and beneath which John Wesley preached. A local legend maintained that the spirit of Maud Toogood, a witch, inhabited the tree and there was a furore when it was decided to fell it after it succumbed to Dutch Elm Disease. It was replaced with an oak tree in 1986. To date, fears over Maud's release into the community have proved unfounded.

South-east of Ramsbury is **Littlecote House**, one of the finest houses in Wiltshire, and indeed one of the finest Tudor mansions in Britain. Domestically, the site is an ancient one, a Roman villa with a fine mosaic floor having been excavated in the grounds. The present house was built on the site of an earlier manor house by the Darrell family. One member of the family in the 16th century, William Darrell, was infamous for his behaviour.

He overspent on the house, but left his debts unpaid, picked fights with most of his neighbours and was a notorious womaniser. A local midwife claimed she had been taken to the house blindfolded and ordered to aid a woman in labour. When the child was born a man immediately threw the child onto the fire. The midwife did not actually name Darrell, and no court case ensued, but it was apparently common knowledge locally that he was both the father – having claimed *droit de seigneur* on a housemaid – and murderer. It was once claimed that the house was haunted by the lady vainly searching for her child and the shrieks of the infant, but that claim seems to have been played down now that the house is a hotel, publicity literature noting only the occasional friendly ghost.

The hotel also claims to be in Berkshire rather than Wiltshire, despite the obvious evidence of the county boundary line on maps: perhaps the Royal county is thought to be a better address. Visitors can still view the house's Great Hall and Long Gallery (almost 110 feet – over 30m – long), both of which are superb. Henry VIII is said to have wooed Jane Seymour here and their initials are entwined in the stained glass of the Great Hall. Visitors to the house can also see a mosaic from the Roman villa. Henry VIII is also remembered at nearby **Chilton Foliat**: this neat little village with its Georgian houses was given by Henry VIII to each of his wives in turn.

From Aldbourne and Ramsbury, country lanes lead west to **Ogbourne St Andrew**, set on the River Og (the Og Bourne), a tributary of the Kennet, a pleasant place with a neat church beside a Jacobean manor house. The lane from Aldbourne passes close to the site of the medieval village of **Snap**. Unlike other downland villages which were deserted when Black Death killed the inhabitants, Snap thrived until a century ago when changes in farming methods, chiefly the replacement of crops with sheep, meant fewer workers were required. In 1907 the last inhabitants left.

Marlborough

South now is **Marlborough**. Some have suggested, disparagingly, that the town is just one long street. There is some truth in this – but what a spectacular street. The town's name derives from the Saxon *Merle Beorg*, 'Merlin's Grave'. The 'grave' was the mound at the western end of the town, in what are now the grounds of Marlborough College. In Norman times this was part of a typical 'motte and bailey' castle, but as the Celtic origin of the name proves, the mound existed before the Norman conquest. Excavations show that the mound pre-dated the Celts too, being a contemporary of Silbury Hill, which lies to the west. The Celtic name for the mound is no surprise, the Celts often linking mythical or legendary heroes with features they did not understand, but the idea that Merlin could lie beneath a mound on the Marlborough Downs is an intriguing link with King Arthur, who may have fought the Saxons on the nearby Downs.

A modification of the old name created the 'borough': perhaps this occurred after it had been granted a charter by King John in 1204. But the town did not forget its link with Arthur's magician, adopting the motto *Ubi Nunc Sapientis Ossa Merlini* – 'where lie the bones of the wise Merlin'.

The Saxon village of Marlborough was sited on what is now **The Green**, at the eastern end of the town. The Normans utilised the mound at the western end, the medieval development of the town linking the two with what is claimed to be the widest high street in Britain. To explore the town, start at The Green. Medieval towns and villages, with their timber-framed, thatched houses, were plagued by fire, the limited firefighting techniques and equipment occasionally allowing fires to spread with disastrous consequences. Marlborough was no exception, a fire in 1653 destroying around 250 houses, a large fraction of the town, and causing such damage that it so impoverished the townsfolk that a subscription was taken up throughout England to enable rebuilding to start. Further fires in 1679 and 1690 were less disastrous, but so fearful did the town council become that following the latter blaze a by-law was passed forbidding the use of thatch as a roofing material. Many of the attractive houses at The Green date from the rebuilding after the 1653 fires, though it is claimed that the cellars in some actually date from the town's Saxon period.

The avenue of lime trees on the far side of The Green was planted in 1840. Beyond it is **Patten Alley**, so called because it was necessary to wear pattens – a shoe or clog, usually set on an iron ring – when taking it on muddy days. A plaque on No. 29, to the right, notes that it was where William Golding,

author of *Lord of the Flies* among other fine novels and winner of the 1983 Nobel Prize for Literature, spent his boyhood; his father taught at the local grammar school, where Golding was educated before going up to Oxford.

Follow the alley to reach **St Mary the Virgin Church**. The church dates from the mid-12th century, but little is Norman, most of the fabric dating from a 15th-century rebuild. In the fire of 1653 St Mary's was gutted and the reddening of the internal stonework is still visible – look, particularly, at the west wall. As you leave the church, look above the porch, to the left, to see some carvings – now very weathered – of cats. A local legend maintains that this commemorates a cat who repeatedly returned to the church tower to rescue her kittens during the 1653 fire. It is a lovely story, but the carvings actually date from the 15th-century rebuild.

Continue along Patten Alley, then bear left to reach the High Street, with the **Town Hall**, built, in fine style, in 1900 to the left. The High Street is a delight, its looks spoiled only by the central car park and the cars lining its pavements. A little way along, to the right, the **Merchant's House** (No. 132) dates from 1656. It was built for Thomas Bayly, a silk merchant who clearly spared no expanse. Inside, the 'Great Parlour' has original full-length oak wall-panelling, while elsewhere there is more original decoration. The house has been restored and furnished in period style.

High Street has some fine buildings, several of which were coaching inns, Marlborough being on the coach route from Bath to London. There are several plaques in High Street. One recalls a Civil War skirmish when a Royalist band broke into the town, while others recall visits to the town by Samuel Pepys, the famous diarist, and the Lord Chamberlain's men. The latter were a 16th-century group of travelling actors who included William Shakespeare among their number. The Men apparently made four visits to the town, though it is not certain that the great man was with them on any of these occasions. At the bottom of High Street another plaque marks the spot where the fire of 1653 began, at the tanning shop of Francis Freeman. Oak bark, used in the tanning process, caught fire, and within three hours the flames, fanned by a strong wind, had virtually destroyed the town. Further on, standing on an island in the wide street is the church of **St Peter and St Paul**, built in the 15th century but remodelled later. Beyond the church is **Marlborough College**. It occupies, in part, a house built in the 17th century by the Duke of Somerset around the mound of the Norman castle. Formerly a public school for boys, it now also takes girl scholars.

From St Peter's Church, walk back along High Street, turn right through the arch to The Priory and walk through the gardens to the bridge over the Kennet. Cross and turn left, following the road to recross the Kennet. At this point there was once a mill, its waterwheel driven by the river, owned by John Churchill, the general whose victory at Blenheim in 1704 over the army of Louis XIV saved Europe from French expansionism. A grateful nation

Cottage near Ogbourne St George

Silbury Hill

gave Churchill the money to build Blenheim Palace near Oxford. John Churchill's father was Sir Winston: one of the later members of the family was a more famous Sir Winston Churchill. John Churchill took the title 1st Duke of Marlborough, in part because of his holdings here which had been inherited from his mother who came from a (defunct) line of Earls of Marlborough.

A short distance west of Marlborough College, turn left for **Preshute** – on the hill to the south is a white horse cut in 1804 by boys from Marlborough School, the predecessor of the College. The figure is actually a very good representation of a horse, but is difficult to see as the ground on which it is cut is at a shallow angle and, from what would be the best vantage points, it tends to be obscured by trees and hedges.

South of Marlborough

South of Marlborough, on the A345 towards Pewsey, is **Oare** where **Oare House**, originally built in 1740, was extended in the 1920s by Clough Williams-Ellis, the builder of Portmeirion in north Wales. Williams-Ellis also built the terrace of cottages at the south end of the village and Cold Blow at the north-western end.

Sandwiched between the other two main roads which head south-east and east from Marlborough (the A338 for Salisbury and the A4 to Hungerford) is **Savernake Forest**, one of the last great forests of southern England and another of the treasures of Wiltshire. After the Conquest, the Norman kings made it a royal hunting preserve, William the Conqueror making Richard Esturmy, who had fought with him at Hastings, the Hereditary Warden of Savernake. From the Esturmys the wardenship passed to the Seymours. It is said that Henry VIII met Jane Seymour after hunting in the forest. From the Seymours the wardenship passed to the Bruces, who became the Earls (later Marquesses) of Ailesbury.

It was the first Marquess who, in 1825, built **Tottenham House**, which lies to the south-east of the forest. The house is now a school, but the church (**St Katherine's**, built by the second Marchioness of Ailesbury in 1861) to the north of the house can be visited. At the end of the **Column Ride** heading north-west from Tottenham House is a column erected by the Earl of Ailesbury in 1781. It is believed that the column previously stood in Hammersmith, London, where it had been erected about 20 years before by a gentleman wishing to commemorate his wife. It is occasionally said that Ailesbury raised the column to commemorate George III's recovery from madness, a somewhat optimistic reason if true. In the 18th century the forest had become overgrown with thickets and Capability Brown was asked to take it in hand. Brown created the Grand Avenue, a 4-mile (6½km) drive – 3½ miles (5½km) of it perfectly straight – from the house through the centre of the forest. At its heart he made a Circus from which eight rides radiate symmetrically. In 1939, the Forestry Commission signed a 999-year lease with the Marquess, making Savernake the only large forest in Britain to be so leased.

With its great oaks – the **Big Belly Oaks** on the west side are said to be centuries old – beech and chestnuts

(but, sadly, no longer any elms) Savernake is a wonderful place to walk and picnic, and a haven for woodland birds and butterflies. For the lucky visitor, there may even be a glimpse of deer whose ancestors were hunted by Henry VIII. The forest is criss-crossed with tracks and paths, but on one day each year these are closed to visitors to stop them becoming established rights of way.

The **Kennett and Avon Canal** makes a splendid curve around the southern tip of the forest. At the hamlet of Crofton, which lies on a Roman road which traversed Savernake, the **Crofton Beam Engines** has two Cornish beam engines (dated 1812 and 1846) which pumped water to the summit level of the canal. When operating, the engines were steamed from a hand-stoked boiler. The 1812 engine is the oldest operating beam engine in the world. Close by is **Wilton**, to the east of which is Wiltshire's only operating windmill, built in 1821 after the Kennet and Avon Canal had taken the water from the River Bedwyn and so prevented watermills from operating. The mill operated until 1920 then fell into disrepair. A rescue operation was mounted in 1971 and the mill was restored in 1976. It is now a local landmark, especially when floodlit during the early evening. Guided tours of the mill are available and flour ground on site can be bought. A fine walk can be followed beside **Wilton Water**, linking the village to the Crofton Beam Engines site.

From Crofton follow the minor road beside the canal to **Great Bedwyn**, where the tomb of Sir John Seymour, the father of Henry VIII's third wife, Jane Seymour, can be found in the church. Sir John was a Warden of Savernake Forest. The church, a fine 12th-century building, also has a brass to an earlier John Seymour and the stone effigy of a knight, probably dating from the early 14th century. The village is famous for its stonemason's, which has been turned into an open-air museum of the craft, with gravestones and other carvings mounted on the walls and in the yard.

To the north of Great Bedwyn, **Chisbury** is a final Wiltshire village. Here there is an old chapel, complete with 13th-century windows, now part of a farm, the whole farm standing within the ramparts and ditches of a late Iron Age hillfort.

Places to Visit

Avebury

Great Barn (National Trust)

Open: Apr–Oct, daily 10am–6pm, Nov–Mar, daily 10am–4pm.
☎ 01672 539250

Alexander Keiller Museum (National Trust)

Open: Apr–Oct, daily 10am–6pm, Nov–Mar, daily 10am–4pm.
☎ 01672 539250

Avebury Manor and Garden (National Trust)

Open: House: Apr–Oct, Mon, Tue and Sun 2–4pm. Garden: Apr–Oct, Sat–Tue, 11am–5pm.
☎ 01672 539250

Marlborough

The Merchant's House

132 High Street
Open: Easter–Sep, Fri and Sat 11am–4pm.
☎ 01672 511491

Ramsbury

Littlecote House

Open: The house is now a hotel, but visitors are allowed at any reasonable time.
☎ 01488 682509

Wilton

Crofton Beam Engines

Kennet and Avon Canal
Open: Easter–Oct, daily 10.30am–5pm. Steaming weekends at various times from Easter to Aug – please ring for exact schedules.
☎ 01672 870300

Wilton Windmill

Open: Easter–Sep. Guided Tours only. Sun 2–5pm, Bank Holiday Mon 2–5pm.
☎ 01672 870202

In this final chapter we start at Trowbridge, the county town of Wiltshire, and end at Salisbury, the county's only city. On the way we skirt Salisbury Plain and visit Stonehenge, two very different survivals from an earlier England.

Trowbridge

Trowbridge has a Saxon name, deriving from 'tree bridge', the bridge crossing the River Biss. After the Saxons came the Normans, who built castle. The castle is long gone, but an excellent model of it can be seen in the town museum. As with all Wiltshire's main towns, Trowbridge grew prosperous on the wool trade, becoming a centre for small manufacturing industries when the trade went into steep decline. The main interest in the town is found close to the old market: in Market Street the **Town Hall**, now occupied by the Magistrates' Courts, is a fine example of Victorian architecture. Behind the Town Hall is the town park, which includes the **Sensory Garden**, a millennium project which incorporates trees, shrubs, flowers and water, to-

gether with sculpture and mosaic to create a feast for the senses.

To the north of the Town Hall, in Fore Street, is the site of the medieval market, close to **St James' Church**, a Norman foundation. On the far side of the church the town **almshouses**, on the corner of Union and Church Street, were built, in elegant style, in the 1860s. To the left, opposite the church, is **The Shires**, the town museum with a collection on Trowbridge's history and an exhibition on Isaac Pitman, the town's most famous son (see feature box). Continuing along Fore Street the visitor passes, to the right, **The Parade**, often claimed to be the finest group of clothiers' houses in the county. The group was carefully restored when it was the headquarters of Ushers Brewery. Further on is the town lock-up or **Blind House** with its curious finial.

Trowbridge to Warminster

South of Trowbridge the A350 takes the visitor speedily to Westbury, though a short detour west is worthwhile to visit the **Brokerswood Country Park** where there are a miniature railway, children's adventure playgrounds and several nature trails through the 80 acres (32 hectares) of broadleaf woodland which makes up a large section of the park.

Westbury is a very pleasant little market town, with some elegant build-ings which reflect the wealth of the wool trade, here as elsewhere. The town church, **All Saints**, is a fine building in perpendicular style. One interesting feature is the Victorian swimming baths, claimed to be the oldest in Britain to be still in use, and perhaps also the only one to have a resident ghost, an amiable spectre who glories in the name of George. As well as having tourist information, the **Westbury Visitor Centre** also has a collection of local historical finds.

Westbury claims to have been the actual site of King Alfred's cake-burning, though as the incident is believed to be a legend rather than a fact, the claim seems optimistic. It is likely to have arisen because of the association of Alfred with the **white horse** to the east of the town, beside the road to Bratton. The present horse, or, at least, its immediate predecessor, dates from 1778, making it the oldest of the Wiltshire horses. What is certain is that there was an earlier form, though the date of this is much debated. Some claim it was carved on Alfred's orders to commemorate his victory over the Norsemen at Ethandun, which most experts consider to mean Edington, the village close to the horse. However, there are some who disagree with the identification of Ethandun as Edington, and many more who consider the idea of a Saxon date for the first carved horse fanciful. Both the Uffington white horse and the Cerne Abbas giant are of the suggested age, so there are precedents for the early date, and the

Isaac Pitman

Isaac Pitman was born in Trowbridge on 4 January 1813. He went to the town's Free School, leaving at 12 years of age to work in one of the local mills as a clerk. He was, however, keen to further his education and in 1831 left the town to train as a teacher in London. After completing his training – in just 5 months – he became a schoolmaster in Barton-on-Humber near Hull. In 1835 he married a local widow, the two of them moving to Wotton-under-Edge in Gloucestershire in 1836, firstly as head of a British School, but later opening his own private school. It was during his time at Wotton that he devised the shorthand method which now bears his name. He sold a pamphlet on his system, though it was many years before it became the established method of shorthand. By then the Pitmans had moved to Bath where they stayed for the remainder of Isaac's long life.

By 1890 it is estimated that over 100,000 people were learning shorthand annually, and the Pitman system is still the major form of shorthand. Isaac was knighted for his work in 1894. He died on 14 January 1897, just a few days after his 84th birthday. The town museum has a collection of memorabilia of Pitman's life and system.

drawing of the earliest horse does bear some similarity to the one at Uffington. Whatever the history of the first horse, what is definite is that the second was carved in 1778 and has been maintained ever since.

The white horse is carved at the edge of an Iron Age hillfort called **Bratton Castle**, at the centre of which is a long barrow. If there was indeed a battle here in 878, the hill has seen important developments in Wiltshire's history over a period of several thousand years. The long barrow is a Neolithic (New Stone Age) burial tomb – of similar age to the more impressive sites in the east of the county. The hillfort has double ramp/ditch defences, placing it later in the Iron Age. Initially such forts had single defences, but the invention of the slingshot made double (or even multiple) defences necessary to keep attackers further back.

Edington, perhaps the site of Alfred's critical victory, is a fine village with a church which Pevsner maintains is both 'wonderful and highly important'. The wonder is the appearance of so large and magnificent a building in a small building. The importance lies in the church's fusion of the Decorated and Perpendicular styles, as the former grew into the latter. In 1351 the Bishop of Winchester decided to build a chantry at Edington, with a church and living accommodation for two priests and a warden. It is clear that what the Bishop had in mind was a cathedral-like church to add majesty to his benevolence. Inside are memorials to one of the original priests (or, more likely, a successor) and several other fine monuments. There are effigies of early 14th-century knights and, best of all, the monument to Sir Edward Lewys and his wife, the pair side by side with an angel hovering above them.

Back at Westbury the main road south soon reaches **Warminster**, which achieved notoriety in the 1960s when a series of UFOs were seen above the town. No satisfactory explanation was ever forthcoming for the sightings and for a while ufologists and others flocked to the town to watch the skies. It is said that it was at the Saxon settlement of Warminster that King Alfred assembled his army before marching to Ethandun to defeat the Norse invaders (though that claim is disputed – see below). Later Warminster was a market town, famous as a centre for wheat trading. Daniel Defoe actually claimed that it was England's premier wheat market, and this feature of the town's past is commemorated in *Beyond Harvest*, a bronze artwork in which a young girl sits on top of a stack of wheat sacks. The work, by Colin Lambert, is rather more eye-catching than the tall obelisk at the junctions of Silver, Vicarage and Church streets which was erected to commemorate the enclosure of the parish in 1781. Look out, too, for the **Grammar School**, built in 1707 by Thomas Thynne, Viscount Weymouth, an ancestor of the present owner of Longleat. One famous pupil was Thomas Arnold, later headmaster of Rugby. The town's history is explored in the **Dewey Museum** in the public library.

South-west Wiltshire

To the east of Warminster is **Cley Hill**, a National Trust site which includes an Iron Age hillfort and two Bronze Age barrows. The hill is an impressive viewpoint and was extremely popular with UFO-watchers in the 1960s. South of the hill is **Longleat**. The house stands on the site of an Augustinian (later Carthusian) Priory. At the Dissolution the entire estate was bought by Sir John Thynne for £53. He lived in the monastery buildings, but gradually rebuilt and extended them; what the visitor now sees is mostly from the mid-16th century, though the work was completed after Thynne's death in 1580. The huge house is in fine Elizabethan style, with a uniform design on all four facades, an unusual feature for the time. The interior is as grand as the exterior with beautiful furnishings and priceless artwork. Longleat is the home of the **Needlecraft Centre**, and there are excellent collections of costume and Flemish tapestries. The house, now the home of the Marquis of Bath, was one of the first of the great stately homes to be opened to the public.

Longleat's gardens are in formal, Italian style, but the parkland was the work of Capability Brown, who spent five years here, from 1757 to 1762. Later the park was remodelled by Humphry Repton. Today the grounds are more famous for the **Safari Park**, one of Britain's first. Vehicles are required if you wish to enter the big cat and other enclosures, but visitors can walk among giraffes, zebras, camels and llamas. The park also has sea lions and gorillas: all the animals have recently become even more famous as a result of TV's *Animal Park*. At the pets' corner children can get much closer to the animals. To complete the attractions there is the world's longest hedge maze, a railway, an adven-

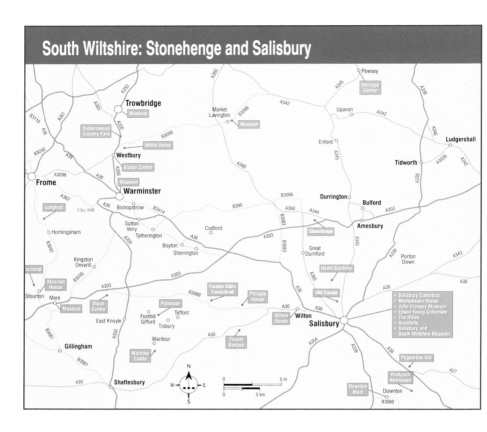

South Wiltshire: Stonehenge and Salisbury

Above: Turf Bridge, Stourbridge

Below: The Parade, Trowbridge, claimed to be the finest clothiers houses in Wiltshire

Opposite page: Longleat House

ture playground and much more.

Longleat is approached from the A362. If instead the visitor heads south along the A350, a right turn at Longbridge Deverill follows either a road through the other Deverill villages, or a road around the boundary of the Longleat estate to reach Alfred's Tower and the other great Wiltshire estate – Stourhead.

The triangular **Alfred's Tower** was erected in 1772 by Henry Hoare, the owner of Stourhead. The tower is 160ft (49m) high and according to local tradition marks the spot where Alfred the Great gathered his army to fight the Norse in 878. As we have seen, this claim is disputed by Warminster, and most expert opinion dismisses both sites in favour of Egbert's Stone, further south. For those willing to climb the tower's tight spiral staircase (of 205 steps) there is a marvellous view westwards across Somerset and over Stourhead itself.

White Sheet Hill

To the north of Mere, White Sheet Hill is topped by a Neolithic causeway camp and several Bronze Age burial mounds. There are also strip lynchets – the ancient form of farming where a field was divided into strips which were allocated to the locals – and pillow mounds, an artificial warren constructed for rabbits, the locals then harvesting the animals at a time when meat was expensive. The hill has a nature trail and is also an excellent viewpoint.

Stourhead, Henry Hoare's house, was one of the first of the great Georgian houses, designed by Colin Campbell and completed in 1722. Hoare, a banker, had bought the estate from the Stourton family, who had owned it since the Norman Conquest. The house was badly damaged by fire in 1902, but rebuilt in fine style. One of the parts most seriously damaged was the library where, legend has it, Edward Gibbon, then aged 14, was inspired to write the *Decline and Fall of the Roman Empire*. The house is superbly furnished, with carved woodwork by Grinling Gibbons, statues by Michael Rysbrack and a fine collection of paintings.

About 20 years after completion of the house, Henry Hoare's son laid out the gardens, adding lakes and temples – a copy of the Roman Pantheon and the Baalbeck Temple of the Sun among others – statues and bridges. The whole is one of the finest 18th-century gardens in Britain, especially pleasing in spring when the azaleas and rhododendrons are in bloom, and in autumn when the beech trees turn to gold. One entrance to the estate – which is now owned by the National Trust – is marked by a late 14th-century High Cross brought here from Bristol. The lower niches of the Cross hold original statues of Kings John, Henry II, Edward III and Edward IV. The upper statues, of Henry VI, Elizabeth I, James I and Charles I were added in 1663.

Close to the Stourhead car park, the flower garden of **Stourton House** is a 4-acre (1.6-hectare) site which, in season, is alive with the colour of hundreds of flowers and shrubs. The garden specialises in the production of dried

William Beckford

William Beckford (1760–1844) was Member of Parliament for Wells, Somerset and for Hindon here in Wiltshire for many years, but is more famous for being a writer and eccentric. His writing included several novels and also travel writing, the latter in part because of a self-imposed exile when gossip surrounded his relationship with Viscount Courtenay, a boy in his early teens. Beckford was married and devoted to his wife (she died in childbirth aged 24 and he never remarried) but he does appear to have been infatuated with the young boy, even if the more scandalous suggestions were unfounded.

Beckford was fascinated by follies. He was responsible for Beckford's Tower near Bath, and at Fonthill Gifford built a house which was to have both inhabitable and ruinous sections. When he first occupied the house he threw a three-day party attended by Lord Nelson and Sir William and Lady Hamilton. Beckford lived at Fonthill Abbey for 16 years, but the building was never completed and largely collapsed two years after he moved out. Today the diligent visitor can search out what little remains. The most impressive section is the gateway, attributed to Inigo Jones.

flowers, which are available for sale.

From Stourton we head east towards Salisbury. The next village is **Mere**, a stone-built village grouped around a fine church. William Barnes, the Dorset dialect poet, was once the schoolmaster here and Charles II stayed at the George Inn while escaping from the battle of Worcester. The **village museum** touches on these and other aspects of local area history with permanent collections and regular exhibitions.

Further east, at **East Knoyle**, a stone monument marks the place where Sir Christopher Wren, the architect of St Paul's Cathedral among other buildings, was born in 1632. Wren's father, also Christopher, was the vicar and was responsible for the plasterwork in the chancel which has delighted visitors for centuries. To the east of the village **Windmill Hill** is surmounted by the

mill of the name, its sails long since gone. A little further east, at Bush Farm, is the **Bison Centre** where herds of both bison and elk can be seen. The animals are farmed, meat products being available. The farm also has rare pig, poultry and sheep breeds, smaller animals such as prairie dogs, chipmunks and raccoons, and owls. There is also a gallery which displays wildlife art by North American artists. The farm's woodland, mainly mature oak, has been laid out with paths and clearings.

South of East Knoyle the A350 crosses the county border into Dorset, soon reaching **Shaftesbury**, famous for Gold Hill, a steep hill of cottages which has appeared in TV adverts. But we head east to **Fonthill Gifford**, where William Beckford built a Palladian mansion, **Fonthill Abbey**, which, in keeping with his style (see feature box), was to be part-house, part-folly.

South of Fonthill Gifford, near Tisbury, **Pythouse** is also Palladian, but rather better constructed than Beckford's folly. The house was built in 1725 on the site of an Elizabethan mansion. The estate surrounding the house was the scene of riots in 1830 when several hundred agricultural workers rioted against their working conditions. The local militia was called and put down the riot. No one was killed, but several of the workers were sentenced to transportation. There is also a curious story associated with the house involving a housemaid called Molly. She was sentenced to death for killing her baby by scalding, but claimed the incident was an accident. There were rumours that the child was fathered by one of the family and that before her execution Molly cursed the family, saying that unless she was buried at Pythouse terrible events would follow. Apparently her bones were kept at the house, and each time there was an attempt to remove them tragedy resulted – there was a serious fire, a son of the family died, and then a daughter as well.

To the south of Pythouse is **Wardour,** which has two castles. The **Old Castle** was built in the 1390s by John, Lord Lovel of Titchmarsh. He had been a soldier during the Hundred Years War and is thought to have been strongly influenced by designs he saw on campaign in France. The castle he built is unique in Britain, with an octagonal tower house built around a hexagonal courtyard. The castle was intended to be a mansion rather than a fortress, but during the Civil War it became the latter in May 1643 when the Royalist Lady Blanche Arundell, in the absence of her husband, defended it with fifty men against a Parliamentary force of well over one thousand. Given the odds the siege was inevitably brief, Lady Blanche surrendering after just six days. In March of the following year the new occupier, Edmund Ludlow, defended the castle against Royalists intent on regaining control. Ludlow held out for ten months, but was eventually forced to surrender. The damage inflicted on the castle during the sieges meant it was never habitable again. Today it is a romantic ruin in the care of English Heritage. With its curious design and fabulous position, on a hill above a small lake, it is a marvellous site.

The second castle at Wardour was built by Lord Arundell about a century after the loss of the old castle. It is a fine Georgian building (the biggest in the county), but is not open to the public.

To the east of Fonthill Gifford are a number of very pretty villages and two interesting visitor sites. **Farmer Giles**, near Teffont Magna, is a 38-acre (15-hectare) farm with animals which children can feed and handle, an alpaca herd and both indoor and outdoor play areas. The farm has an excellent restaurant and is home to the Wiltshire Wildlife Rescue Hospital. On the eastern side of Teffont Magna is **Philipps House**, built in the early 19th century in Grecian style for the politician William Wyndham. The Ionic portico is terrific, while inside there is a fine grand staircase and an impressive collection of Regency furnishings. Surrounding the house is the extensive and beautiful **Dinton Park**, which can be explored. Both the house and park are owned by the National Trust.

South of Teffont, near **Fovant** a series of regimental insignia have, over time, been cut into the steep hillside of Fovant Down. The first badges and emblems were cut during the First World War when soldiers were camped locally. Some of the early figures – including a map of Australia and a kangaroo cut by Australian troops – have not survived but a dozen or so are still visible from the A30. Fovant Down forms part of an extension of Dorset's Cranborne Chase into Wiltshire. Though narrow, the downland is long, extending from Berwick St John in the west all the way to Wilton, and a bridleway runs the whole length, on the downland crest. Along the way there are several interesting sites, with prehistoric ditches, long barrows and Bronze Age sites. One of the better sites is **Chiselbury Camp**, a hillfort close to the Fovant badges. The camp is a wonderful viewpoint of the Nadder valley and southern Wiltshire.

Wilton

Wilton was once the capital of Wessex, but nothing now remains to remind the visitor of this illustrious past. King Alfred founded a Benedictine Nunnery here and later there were other benefactions, a house for Dominican friars and a hospital for several knightly orders being added. These, too, have all gone, the town church dating only from the 1840s. When the nunnery – which had 80 nuns at its height – was dissolved in 1544 the Earl of Pembroke obtained the estate and constructed a house which incorporated very little of the original buildings. Later earls added to **Wilton House** so that little also

now remains of the first Earl's work. However, the later works have created a magnificent building, one of the best in England. Inside, the state rooms include the Inigo Jones' famed 'Double Cube', which is often claimed to be the finest state room in the country. The furnishings and artwork in the house are of the highest quality, particularly the series of paintings by Van Dyck. Outside, the 21 acres (8.5 hectares) of parkland are equally impressive, with water and rose gardens, and including a Palladian bridge. The old riding school buildings have been converted into a Tudor Kitchen and Victorian Laundry to add a neat historical touch, while children will enjoy the adventure playground.

During the medieval period Wilton was famous for its annual sheep fairs and is still a centre for the sheep trade. Later, the opening of the Wilton carpet factory brought added prosperity. Part of the old factory is now occupied by the **Wilton Shopping Village**, which has a carpet factory outlet as well as outlets for leading brands of household and clothing manufacturers. In the town, the **church**, built in the mid-19th century in florid Romanesque style, is extraordinary.

From Wilton it is just a short step to Salisbury.

Salisbury Plain

Salisbury Plain is the largest chalk plateau in Britain, though its actual size depends on precisely where its boundaries are drawn as chalk downland starts in Dorset and continues into Berkshire. Usually the Plain is defined as extending over about 300 square miles (almost 800 sq km), but figures of up to 400 square miles (over 1,000 sq km) are often seen. Historically the Plain was extremely important, several thousand Neolithic, Bronze Age and Iron Age sites having been identified, with further evidence of Roman and Saxon occupation. Of the prehistoric remains the most famous is, of course, Stonehenge, a monument which ranks with the greatest from anywhere in the world.

In Saxon times there were settlements in the river valleys at the Plain edge, the downland being farmed, chiefly on the valley sides where there is often evidence of strip lynchets, while the higher ground was used for sheep rearing. Sheep rearing was the basis of the county's prosperity in the medieval period, the abundance of fine buildings and the spire of Salisbury Cathedral a testament to the wealth sheep – or, rather, wool – brought. The wool trade was in decline, as were the county's fortunes, when the military took an interest in the Plain. The first exercises took place in 1898 after an initial purchase of land the previous year (at about the same time as Guglielmo Marconi was conducting his first experiments on radio on the Plain). Over time the War Department (now the Ministry of Defence) increased its holding: today it owns 150 square miles (390 sq km or 94,000 acres), an area known as Army Training Estate Salisbury Plain (ATE SP). One of the more controversial of the areas acquired was that around the village of **Imber**. The land was bought in the early 1930s, but in 1943, as part of the training programme for the D-Day landings, the villagers were evacuated.

The villagers have never been allowed to return although every year a service is held in the village church.

Around the Plain barracks and related services have grown up. These include the **Boscombe Down** airfield, as military aircraft from all three services use the airspace above the Plain for training. Other NATO forces also train here. Also on the Plain is the Defence Science and Technology Laboratory at **Porton Down**, a secret and controversial establishment. Live firing occurs on about 340 days annually. Visitors using the cross-Plains roads may see tanks and other military vehicles, as these use Plains tracks which occasionally cross the public roads.

Whatever the view taken of the military presence on the Plain, what cannot be denied is that it has prevented the intensive agriculture of a desirable section of land, and that has resulted in the conservation of rare flora and fauna on the calcareous grassland. Of particular note are the breeding of stone curlews, a very rare UK nesting species, on the Plain and the re-introduction of the great bustard, a former British species which became extinct in the wild in 1832. The introduction has gone well. The first eggs were laid in 2007, though these proved to be infertile, almost certainly because the male bird was immature, male great bustards not reaching maturity until they are 4 or 5 years old. In the following winter (2007/8) birds were seen away from the Plain (for instance one near the Severn estuary), raising hopes that they would return to the Plain and attempt to breed again.

Four roads cross the Plain, all of them

Walking on Salisbury Plain

Of the military holding, about 30 per cent is permanently closed to public access. On the rest there is a presumption of right of access, but there are occasions when the need for training overrides this right. Access on the allowed land is on public rights of way only: there is no right-to-roam on the military land. Around Imber, on the western side of the Plain, the Imber Range Perimeter Path has been designated. It is well waymarked and visits a host of interesting sites, offering excellent views. In addition to adherence to the Country Code, walkers on the Plain, for their own safety:

- Should not approach, touch or pick up any objects seen on the ground
- Should keep to footpaths, never deviating from them
- Should never use metal detectors
- Should keep away from all buildings, bunkers and military installations unless clear indications suggest access is permitted
- Should not camp or light fires

For further information on any aspect of access to the Plain, contact:

Headquarters ATE SP, Westdown Camp, Tilshead, Salisbury, SP3 4RS, ☎ 01980 620819

Headquarters Army Training Estate, Land Warfare Centre, Warminster, Wiltshire, BA12 0DJ, ☎ 01985 222856

Defence Estates, Blakemore Drive, Sutton Coldfield, West Midlands, B75 7RL, ☎ 0121 311 2000

For information on live firing, ☎ 01980 674763

---

heading for Salisbury. To the west the old A36 (now the B3414) runs south-east from Warminster, with a minor road linking excellent villages running parallel to it. On the northern side of the main road are two fine hillforts. That on **Battlesbury Hill** has a double ditch/rampart on its steep, south-west, side, and triple defences on the shallower western side. The excavated finds from the site are in Devizes Museum. The fort on **Scratchbury Hill** is less impressive, but the name is interesting, deriving from 'scratch', an old West Country name for the Devil. Several of the villages are also noteworthy. **Bishopstrow** is named for a miracle which occurred when St Aldhelm (Bishop of Malmesbury) visited. He put his staff onto the ground and it immediately took root and grew. A church was built where the miracle occurred, the present church occupying the same site.

At **Boyton** the church has the effigy

Sherrington

of Sir Alexander Giffard, his legs crossed and an otter at his feet. Could the otter commemorate his feat of swimming across the Nile as one of the few survivors of the Battle of Mansourah during the Seventh Crusade in 1249? **Sherrington** has thatched cottages and ducks on a former cress bed, an idyllic spot. The village church is dedicated to St Cosmas and St Damian, two Middle-Eastern saints. It is a very rare dedication, only three other churches in Britain sharing it. **Codford** is interesting for sadder reasons. Australian and New Zealand troops were brought here from 1916 to recover from wounds received in the trenches, and for rehabilitation so they could be sent back to the Front. Australian forces were also stationed at the village. The presence of these men, far from home, explains the Anzac war graves in the village: it is the second largest such cemetery in Britain. It also explains the badge carved on **Lamb Down**, the rising sun being the General Service Badge of Australian

forces. There are also Anzac graves in the churchyard at **Sutton Veny**.

The second road, the A360, heads south from Devizes, passing close to **Market Lavington**, with a history of sheep fairs, wheat trading, brewing and brick making. The town's **museum**, in a house built in the 1840s, has a recreated Victorian kitchen and a collection that covers the more recent history of the town. To the south, **Tilshead** is the headquarters of the military presence on Salisbury Plain. Further on, church lovers will want to visit **Orcheston** and **Maddington**, where there are fine buildings.

The third road traversing the Plain is the best known as it passes close to **Stonehenge**, Wiltshire's most famous ancient monument. The A345 heads south from Marlborough, soon reaching Pewsey, the main town of the **Vale of Pewsey**. The Vale lies west of the town; in the early 19th century William Cobbett journeyed through this area, writing about it in his *Rural Rides*, which was published in 1830. Cobbett liked the Vale, noting the 'villages, hamlets, large forms, towers, steeples, fields, meadows, orchards and very fine timber trees scattered over the valley'. It has changed little, still being a pastoral landscape. The villages that make up the Vale are invariably pretty, and often have interesting churches. Those at **Chirton** and **Marden** have fine Norman doorways. The Marden doorway includes what may be the original door, making it one of the oldest in Britain.

Pewsey is a pleasant market town with a statue of King Alfred gazing across the River Avon. The statue was erected to commemorate the coronation of George V in 1911. To the south of the town there is another white horse, carved in 1937 by the local fire brigade to celebrate another coronation, that of George VI. A little below and to the right of the horse there is (or was) another, carved in 1785, of which nothing can now be seen. The **Pewsey Heritage Centre**, housed in an old foundry, has a collection largely devoted to the Victorian town, including items of industrial and agricultural machinery for the period. The town's Carnival is claimed to be the oldest in Wiltshire.

To the south of Pewsey, **Upavon** is the first substantial village on the River Avon, set where the river is beginning to make its presence felt in the county – more river than stream here, and increasingly so to the south as it flows past a succession of pretty villages: East Chisenbury, Fittleton, Netheravon and Figheldean. **Durrington** is a bigger village, with the stump of an old cross.

Nearby are two prehistoric sites which the visitor can view before moving on to Stonehenge. **Durrington Walls** is a large circular earthwork dating from the Neolithic period, just south of the A345/A3028 roundabout. The site has been heavily farmed, and the main road has been driven through it, so there is little to see, but it is believed that it was an early henge site. Henges are large circular sites, formed by a ditch and wall – similar, therefore, to hillforts, but not placed in defensible positions and with the ditch/wall not high enough to be defensive. Inside the henge there would have been circular wooden buildings and, often, a stone circle. The site was reached through a specific entrance. It is believed that the sites were for ritual or ceremonial purposes.

The second site is **Woodhenge**. Within the henge here there were six concentric circles formed by wooden posts. It is thought the posts may have held aloft a roof. Today the position of the posts is indicated by short concrete pillars. At the centre of the site was the burial of a young child.

It is conjectured that the two henges were forerunners, perhaps even models, for Stonehenge. Indeed, Woodhenge is aligned to the midsummer sunrise and is also about the same diameter as Stonehenge. The vastly more impressive Stonehenge is reached by turning right onto the A303 before Amesbury is reached.

Stonehenge and Amesbury

Stonehenge is arguably the finest prehistoric site in Europe and one of the most impressive ancient sites in the world, as much for its stones as for the enigma surrounding them. The labour of constructing the site was enormous, and with its changes of design Stonehenge was in use for centuries. Exactly what was it for and why was it built here? It is likely that, in the absence of any written record from the builders, we will never know all of the answers, but science has supplied many clues and provided a compelling story.

It is believed that the first henge site, a large earthwork as at Durrington Walls, was constructed in 3100BC. At the same time the Aubrey holes – named for John Aubrey, the 17th-century antiquarian – a ring of steep-sided holes about 3ft (1m) in diameter and 3ft deep, were dug. In some of these cremated remains have been found. The site was then apparently abandoned for around 1,000 years. In 2150BC the second phase of construction began. Eighty-two 'bluestones' were transported from the Preseli Mountains in south-west Wales, 240 miles (almost 400km) from the site. Legend has them flown here by Merlin, science offering the more prosaic, but more likely, explanation of sea and river transport, with the final distance covered by hauling the stones on a rolling road of wooden poles. A stone circle of bluestones was erected.

About 150 years later sarsen stones were brought from near Avebury, where they are found in large numbers. These stones, the largest of which weighs 50 tons, must also have been dragged to the site. It is estimated that to pull such a stone 500 men would have been needed, with a further 100 or so to move the wooden rollers. Even more astonishingly, the sarsens were arranged

in a circle linked by continuous lintel stones. The uprights and lintels had crude mortise and tenon joints hammered from the rock to ensure a snug fit on the uprights. There were also tongue and groove joints hammered out to ensure an equally snug fit between the lintels. The actual method of raising both the massive uprights and the lintels is still debated. Earth ramps would have been the easiest method, but there is no evidence of them. Rather, it is thought, the uprights were pulled into the hole in which they sit, then hauled upright, the lintels being raised by jacking them up on a rising mass of poles. Inside the continuous sarsen circle five trilithons (two uprights with a lintel between them) were erected in a horseshoe. In a final phase, the bluestones were moved to form another circle and horseshoe.

As well as the massive stones, there are also other holes and earth structures which suggest intermediate phases of construction or, perhaps, additional parts of the monument. These merely add to the enigma. Of the purposes of the monument little is known. There are suggestions that the Aubrey holes may have been used to predict eclipses, and various astronomical alignments have been proposed. The only certain one appears to be the alignment with midsummer sunrise where, from the centre of the site, the sun rises above the **Heel Stone**, which is set away from the stone circles, to the north-east. The name 'heel' may derive from an old legend that the Devil built the circle and claimed that no one would ever discover its secrets. When a local monk told the Devil he was wrong, the Devil threw one last stone at him, striking the monk on the heel. More likely the name is from the Celtic *heol*, meaning 'road' or 'way'. One stone at the centre of the monument is known as the Altar Stone, while another further out has been called the Slaughter Stone. There is no evidence to support either name: they just seem to be stones which have fallen over.

Until not so many years ago visitors could wander among the stones, but casual vandalism has meant the erection of a fence. This has been deplored as the true scale of the stones is much more obvious on closer inspection. A more obvious problem for the site is the nearness of the main road – indeed, of the two main roads, as the A303 and A344 split close to the site, enclosing it between them. There have been proposals to put the A344 into a tunnel. That would allow the site to be seen in its correct context, but in December 2007 the proposal, as with all its predecessors, was cancelled because of the expense. For such a magnificent site, of world importance, the idea that it should not be enhanced because of lack of money seems shameful.

Close to Stonehenge there are a host of prehistoric sites, burial mounds and strange ditches. **The Cursus**, to the north, is a pair of parallel earthworks which is not understood. There is also **The Avenue**, also parallel earthworks which seem to link the Heel Stone with the River Avon and may have been used during the construction phase. Interesting prehistoric finds are also associated with nearby **Amesbury**. The town, once famous for the manufacture of clay smoking pipes, is reputedly both the birthplace and burial place of Ambrosius Aurelianus, the leader of the Romano-British against the invading Saxons in the 5th century AD. The town's name is said to derive from this association – this was *Ambrosburh*, Ambrosius' fortress. An abbey for Benedictine nuns was founded at the town in 980, too late for the legend that one of its nuns was Guinevere, who retired here after the death of Arthur. The story is, though, a neat association with the real Ambrosius and the Arthur of legend, who may well have been a British general fighting the Saxons, and there is some evidence for an earlier religious house. After the abbey was dissolved the buildings were inhabited, but gradually decayed and were finally pulled down in 1830 when the present building on the site was erected. There are some good Georgian buildings in the town. To the west of the town, on the way to Stonehenge, on both sides of the A303 the **Trafalgar Clumps** are a group of beech trees planted in the formation of the British and French ships at the Battle of the Nile. It is said they were planted at the request of Lady Hamilton on land belonging to her friend, Baron Amesbury.

South of Amesbury, **Heale Gardens** at **Middle Woodford** occupy an 8-acre (3-hectare) site around a much-modified 17th-century house. It is said that Charles II hid in the house in 1651. The garden is well known for its fantastic snowdrops and aconites in the early year, and for cyclamen and viburnums in summer. The Japanese Garden is excellent. South again is Old Sarum.

Old Sarum has a long and varied history. It began as an Iron Age hillfort, a large one enclosing almost 30 acres

The Druids and Stonehenge

The Druids were the priest class of the Celts. Little is known of their rituals as the Celts had no written language, their history being passed between the generations by oral tradition, which did not survive too well the onslaught of the Romans. The Druids themselves died out at much the same time. There are now Druids again and it is assumed by most people that they have a link with the ancient Druids. Sadly this is not the case. It all started in London in 1792 when the Gentleman's Magazine recorded that on 23 September, 'This being the day on which the autumnal equinox occurred, some Welsh Bards, resident in London, assembled in congress … according to ancient usage … a circle of stones formed, in the middle of which was the Maen Gorsedd, or altar…'

This conclave was organized by Edward Williams, a Glamorgan stonemason living in London. Williams had an interest in Welsh culture, history and poetry. He adopted the bardic title Iolo Morgannwg, and by skilful forgery produced documents which 'proved' that the Glamorgan bards had preserved ceremonies of the original druids. Such forgeries, and the strange ritual of the Gorsedd, would have had little impact on Welsh tradition had Williams not managed to persuade the organizers of the Eisteddfod – then going through a period of decline – that the fake ceremony was real and a necessary addition to their assembly. Consequently the Gorsedd is now set up at a site a year and a day before the Eisteddfod for the ritual pronunciation. The ceremony, because of Williams' forgeries, is inexorably tied up with the Druids, and is therefore carried out by 'Druidic' figures in full regalia. Since no writings or pictures of the Druids are extant the regalia is pure invention consisting of oak leaves, various sceptres and some jewellery based on that of the Bronze Age (i.e. pre-druid).

Nor are the Gorsedd druids the only group claiming descent from the Celtic priesthood, there having been a number set up, mainly during the Victorian revival of interest in prehistory. None has any better, or worse, claim than the Welsh group and in general true historical perspective has been clouded by their activities, particularly their bogus rites at Stonehenge, which pre-dates the original Druids by at least 2,000 years, probably more. The Welsh Eisteddfod (the plural is Eisteddfodau) is a genuinely ancient and worthwhile gathering involving musical and literary competition and, more recently, cultural exchange. It is sad that it has become embroiled in such a collection of bogus rites. It is sad too that the 'Druids' are allowed access to Stonehenge at the midsummer sunrise to perform equally bogus rites while other 'Earth Magic' adherents, whose claim to the site is just as strong, are kept away.

(12 hectares). The fort was probably occupied when the Romans arrived, and they may have made use of it. Four Roman roads met close to the site and Roman *Sorviodunum* was probably within, or incorporated, the fort. The site was certainly occupied by the Saxons, probably after being the scene of a battle against the British in AD552. Later the Saxons had a settlement within the existing ramparts, perhaps recutting the ditches and improving the ramparts. The Normans took the site over and it developed into a medieval town, with substantial buildings and a cathedral. However, as the population expanded the lack of an on-site water supply became acute, and in the early 13th century it was decided to abandon Old Sarum in favour of New Sarum – what was to become the city of Salisbury.

West of Salisbury Plain

The final road crossing Salisbury Plain is the A338 from Marlborough. A left turn off this visits **Ludgershall**. There was a Norman castle here, and the remains of the keep and substantial earthworks are still visible at the northern end of the village. Later, the village was an important local market, and the old market cross can still be seen. There are interesting 17th-century almshouses close to the old castle, while the church, an impressive flint and rubble Early English building, has a monument which Pevsner considered the most important of its age in England. It is dedicated to Richard Brydges (who died in 1558) and his wife. The tomb/

monument is decorated with heraldic symbols, mythical beasts and carved foliage.

The main road passes through the army town of Tidworth, continuing across the A303 to **Boscombe**. On the down to the west was the grave site of the **Boscombe Bowmen**. Seven people (three men, three children and a teenager) were found in the grave, a very unusual number, together with flint arrowheads (hence the name). The grave has been dated to about 2300BC, making the Bowmen contemporaries (or nearly so) with the Amesbury Archer (see feature box). Beyond Boscombe the main road passes close to the Porton Down research station before reaching Salisbury.

South of Salisbury

All the cross-Plain roads have now been explored as far as Salisbury, but before visiting the city we will first head south of it. Close to the A338 towards Fordingbridge, at Downton, **Downton Moot** has an interesting history. It was originally a motte and bailey castle, surrounded by an earthwork which enclosed 10 acres (4 hectares). The keep and other internal defences were of wood. The castle was built by the Bishop of Winchester in the early 12th century and later saw action in a conflict between rival local lords. It was largely destroyed in the late 12th century. The adjacent **Moot House**, a very pretty house, was built in about 1700. The house owners then landscaped the old castle site, adding some follies. In 1972, house and castle became separated, the latter falling into disrepair until a trust was set up

The Amesbury Archer

In May 2002 an early Bronze Age burial was discovered close to Amesbury and Stonehenge. The burial is the richest to have been discovered to date and the man interred at the site was rapidly dubbed 'The King of Stonehenge' by the Press, though there is no proven connection with the site. It is, however, the case that the man belonged to the Beaker people, so called because of their use of a particularly shaped vessel, who have been associated with Stonehenge. Radiocarbon dating suggests the man died around 2500–2100BC. A number of stone arrowheads were found in the grave, this explaining the current nickname, 'The Amesbury Archer'. The grave contained the earliest gold items known in Britain and it is conjectured that the richness of the grave was because the man was a very early metalworker. A second, much less richly endowed burial from the same period has been found nearby.

to renovate the site. It is now open to visitors and is a delight.

At nearby **Redlynch**, the **Newhouse** is 16th century, two wings having been added in the 18th century to produce an unusual design, the three wings forming a Y around a hexagonal central section. The house is extremely attractive and has some interesting decoration and artwork, including a collection of Nelson memorabilia: the daughter of one owner was related to Nelson by marriage and Nelson's daughter by Lady Hamilton was raised at the Newhouse. One early owner of the property was Sir Robert Eyre, the Lord Chief Justice, who was responsible for the Pepperbox which names **Pepperbox Hill**, a National Trust site on the A36 which heads from Salisbury towards Southampton. The **Pepperbox**, also called **Eyre's Folly**, is a curious octagonal brick building. The National Trust site which surrounds it covers about 70 acres (28 hectares) of down and woodland and is a marvellous viewpoint. On clear days the Isle of Wight is visible (or so it is said!).

Salisbury

Salisbury is one of England's finest small cities, its magnificent cathedral the centre of a Close that is a haven of calm just a few metres from the frantic haste of the ring road. As we have seen, the city grew up after the abandonment of Old Sarum. The cathedral was one of the first buildings to have been constructed on the new site, though others soon followed. As elsewhere, the presence of a cathedral aided the growth and prosperity of the surrounding city. To this was added the wealth of the medieval wool trade, Salisbury being a major centre. Today the city has maintained many of its medieval and later buildings, merging the needs of a major conurbation with the need to retain the essence of its origins. As a consequence any walk reveals much of interest.

But all walks should start at the **cathedral**. It was begun in 1220 by Bishop Richard Poore after, legend has it, the site was chosen by an archer who shot an arrow from Old Sarum when the decision to move was made. The cathedral was completed in 1258, a soaring building, a masterpiece of the stonemason's art. Although 38 years is a long time, it was short enough for the style of the building to be entirely Early English. Because of this unity, many experts believe that the cathedral is the finest in England. Inside, be sure to look at the Purbeck marble pillars which carry the spire. The spire is 404 feet (123m) tall, the highest in England, and is set on a magnificent tower. The original design was for a small lantern tower and it was for that the pillars were installed. Standing below them, the distinct bow caused by the massive weight they are carrying can easily be seen. At the west end of the church, the medieval clock, constructed in 1386, is the oldest in Britain and among the oldest in the world. At the other end is a superb revolving glass prism engraved by Lawrence Whistler. Between the two are a number of excellent tombs; indeed, so fine are the tombs and monuments that an entire chapter, perhaps even a book, could be devoted to them. The cathedral also has wonderful cloisters (though it was never part of a monastery), planted (in 1837, to commemorate Queen Victoria's accession) with cedars of Lebanon. In the **Chapter House** some of the cathedral's treasures are on display. These include one of only four surviving versions of **Magna Carta**. Salisbury's version is actually the best of the four, being virtually undamaged.

The cathedral stands in **Cathedral Close**, arguably the most beautiful Close in England. Originally a cemetery, the graves were moved in the 18th century, the ground being levelled and lawned. At the north-west corner is the late medieval **North Gate**. Close by is **Mompesson House**, built for a rich merchant (whose tomb lies within the cathedral) in the early 18th century. Next south is **The Rifles** (formerly Redcoats in the Wardrobe), the Regimental Museum of the Royal Gloucestershire, Berkshire and Wiltshire Regiment and predecessor regiments. The name 'The Wardrobe' derives from the building's former use as the Bishop's clothing storeroom.

Southwards is **Arundells**, formerly the home of Sir Edward Heath, which can be visited by appointment during the summer. Next is the **King's House**, originally built at the same time as the cathedral, but rebuilt in the 15th century. This wonderful building now houses the **Salisbury and South Wiltshire Museum**, with exhibits on Stonehenge, Old Sarum and the history of Salisbury. There are also collections of costume, lace and embroidery, ceramics and paintings.

Now walk past the cathedral (with it on your right) to reach the 14th-century **St Anne's Gate**. To the right are the Deanery and, beyond, Bishop Wordsworth's School. Go through the Gate: the wall to the right, enclosing the Close, is contemporary with the Gate, the latter giving access through it. Turn left along St John's Street, then left again along New Street. At its end a left turn will return you to North Gate.

In the town, be sure to visit the **Market Square** with its marvellous timber-framed and Georgian buildings. On the southern side are Butcher Row, with its gabled houses, and Fish Row,

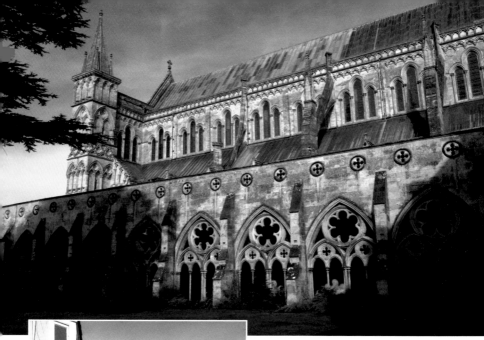

Above: Salisbury Cathedral
Left: Northgate, Salisbury

named for the merchants which once occupied them At the western end of Butcher Row is the 15th-century **Poultry Cross**, which continues the merchandise theme, as does Oatmeal Row and Cheese Market on the west side of the Market Square. Silver Street, a continuation of Butcher Row, also has fine gabled houses. Blue Boar Row on the north side of Market Square seems more likely to have been named for an inn than an animal. At the corner of it and the quaintly-named Endless Street is a superb 14th-century gabled, tile-hung building. At the other end of Blue Boar Row, the public library houses two small museums, the **Edwin Young Collection** of 19th- and 20th-century paintings of Salisbury and the local area, and the **John Creasey Museum**, with books and memorabilia of the famous crime writer.

This description of the centre of Salisbury has been necessarily brief, but please explore further afield: as well as fine buildings the city has two excellent theatres and an arts centre which hosts theatre, music and dance.

Places to Visit

Trowbridge

Town Museum

The Shires, Court Street
Open: All year, Tue–Fri 10am–4pm,
Sat 10am–5pm.
☎ 01225 752339

Brokerswood Country Park

Open: All year, daily 10am–5pm (4pm
Nov–Mar). Closed on Christmas Day,
Boxing Day and New Years' Day.
☎ 01373 822238

Westbury

Visitor Centre

Open: All year, Tue, Thu and Fri
10am–4pm, Sat 10am–1pm.
☎ 01373 825784

Warminster

Dewey Museum

Public Library, Three Horseshoes
Walk, Warminster
Open: All year, Mon and Tue 10am–
5pm, Wed 10am–1pm, Thu and Fri
10am–7pm, Sat 9am–4pm. Closed
on Bank Holidays.
☎ 01985 216022

Longleat

Open: House: Nov–mid-Feb, daily
11am–3pm. Mid-Feb–Oct, daily
10am–5pm (5.30pm at weekends).
Safari Park: mid-Mar–Oct, daily
10am–4pm (5pm at weekends, Bank
Holidays and school holidays). All
other attractions: mid-Mar–Oct,

daily 11am–5pm (10.30am–5.30pm
at weekends, Bank Holidays and
school holidays).
☎ 01985 844400

Stourhead (National Trust)

Open: Alfred's Tower: mid-Mar–
Oct, daily 11.30am–4.30pm. House:
mid-Mar–Oct, Fri–Tue 11.30am–
4.30pm. Park: All year, daily 9am–
7pm.
☎ 01747 841152

Stourton House Flower Garden

Stourton
Open: Apr–Nov, Wed, Thu, Sun and
Bank Holiday Mons 11am–6pm or
dusk.
☎ 01747 840417

Mere

Town Museum

Public Library and Information
Centre, Mere
Open: All year, Mon 10am–7pm,
Tue–Fri 9am–5pm, Sat 9am–1pm.
Closed on Bank Holidays.
☎ 01747 860908

Bison Centre and Woodland Gardens

Bush Farm, Mere
Open: Apr–Sep, Wed–Sun 10am–
5pm. Also open on Bank Holidays.
☎ 01747 830263

Places to Visit

Tisbury

Pythouse

Tisbury
Open: May–Sep, daily 2–4.30pm.
☎ 01747 870210

Old Wardour Castle (English Heritage)

Wardour
Open: Apr–Oct, daily 10am–5pm
(closes at 6pm in Jul and Aug, and
at 4pm in Oct). Nov–mid-Mar, Sat and
Sun 10am–4pm.
☎ 01747 870487

Teffont

Farmer Giles Farmstead

Open: All year, daily 10am–6pm.
Closed Christmas Day and Boxing
Day.
☎ 01722 716338

Philipps House and Dinton Park (National Trust)

Open: House: mid-Mar–Oct, Mon
1–5pm, Sat 10am–1pm. Park: All
year, daily 10am–5pm.
☎ 01722 716663

Wilton

Wilton House

Open: House: Easter and Apr–
Aug, Sun–Thu and Bank Holidays
12noon–5pm. Sep Tue–Thu 12noon–
5pm. Park: Easter and Apr–Sep, daily
11am–5.30pm.
☎ 01722 746720

Market Lavington

Town Museum

Church Street
Open: May–Oct, Wed–Sun 2.30–
4.30pm. Also open on Bank
Holidays.
☎ 01380 816222/818736

Pewsey

Pewsey Heritage Centre

Whatleys Old Foundry
Avonside, Pewsey
Open: Apr–Oct, Mon–Fri 10am–4pm,
Sat 10am–12.30pm.
Please note: at the time of writing the
museum is scheduled for closure
in 2008.
☎ 01672 562617

Stonehenge (English Heritage)

Open: mid-Mar–May and Sep–
mid-Oct, daily 9.30am–6pm. Jun–
Aug 9am–7pm. Mid-Oct–mid-Mar
9.30am–4pm (but opens 10am on
Boxing Day and New Year's Day).
Closed Christmas Eve and Christmas
Day.
☎ 0870 3331181
The National Trust have guided
walks from the Stonehenge car park
around the local prehistoric sites.
These start at 2pm on Saturdays
from May to October. Booking is
essential. ☎ 01672 539167.

Salisbury

Cathedral and Chapter House

Open: Cathedral: All year, daily 7.15am–6.15pm (7.15pm Mon–Sat in Jul and Aug). Chapter House: All year, daily 9.30am–5.30pm (7.45pm Mon–Sat in July and August).
☎ 01722 555120

Mompesson House (National Trust)

Cathedral Close
Open: Easter–Oct, Sat–Wed 11am–5pm. Open on Good Friday.
☎ 01722 335659

The Rifles

58 Cathedral Close
Open: Apr–Oct, daily 10am–5pm, Feb, Mar and Nov, Tue–Sun 10am–5pm.
☎ 01722 419419

Arundells

59 Cathedral Close
Open: Easter–Sep, Sat–Tue 1–5.50pm. Guided tours only. Tours last 45mins and should be booked in advance.
☎ 01722 326546

Salisbury and South Wiltshire Museum

65 Cathedral Close
Open: All year, Mon–Sat 10am–5pm. Also open Sun in Jul and Aug 2–5pm. Closed at Christmas.
☎ 01722 332151

Edwin Young Collection

Public Library, Market Place
Open: All year, Mon 10am–7pm, Tue, Wed and Fri 9am–5pm.
☎ 01722 324145

John Creasey Museum

Public Library, Market Place
Open: All year, Mon 10am–7pm, Tue, Wed and Fri 9am–5pm.
☎ 01722 324145

Heale Gardens

Middle Woodford
Open: All year, daily 10am–5pm. Closed on Bank Holidays.
☎ 01722 782504

Old Sarum (English Heritage)

Open: Jan, Feb, Nov and Dec, daily 11am–3pm. Mar, daily 10am–4pm. Easter or Apr–Sep, daily 10am–5pm (opens at 9am in Jul and Aug).
☎ 01722 335398

Downton Moot

Downton
Open: All year, any reasonable time.
☎ 01725 510039/510762

Redlynch Newhouse

Redlynch
Open: Mar, Mon–Fri 2–5.30pm. Also open at Easter and certain Bank Holidays. Telephone for details.
☎ 01725 510055

Salisbury Cathedral

Attractions for Children

Some attractions have been mentioned in the text. Here, these and some others have been gathered together for convenience.

Boomerang Play Centre
The Outback, Merlin Way
Bowerhill, Melksham
Open: All year, Mon–Fri 9.30am–6pm, Sat 10am–7pm, Sun 10am–6pm.
Tel: 01225 702000
Indoor play with slides, rope bridges and much more. Very good area for young children.

Bowood Adventure Playground
Open: Saturday closest to 1 Apr–Oct, daily 11am–6pm.
Tel: 01249 812102
Soft play area for younger children, adventure playground which includes a life-size pirate ship for older ones.

Butterfly Worl
Studley Grange Garden and Leisure ParkHay Lane, WroughtonOpen: All year, daily except Christmas Day, 10am–6pm (Sun 5pm) or dusk. Last admission 30 minutes before closing.
Tel: 01793 852400
Walk freely among hundreds of the world's most beautiful butterflies and moths, and admire or be terrified by other, equally spectacular, insects.

Cholderton Charlie's Farm
Amesbury Road
Cholderton, nr Salisbury
Open: Easter–Halloween half-term, daily 10am–6pm (close at 4pm early and late in the season)
Tel: 01980 629438
Rare breeds farm where animals can be seen and handled. Rabbit World, Adventure playground, play barn, climbing wall and pig racing.

Coral Cove
Hopton Park
London Road, Devizes
Open: All year, Mon–Thu 9.30am–6pm, Fri and Sat 9.30am–7pm, Sun 10am–5pm.
Tel: 01380 739944
Indoor play with slides, ball pools, mazes and aerial cableways.

Farmer Giles
Teffont
Open: All year, daily 10am–6pm. Closed Christmas Day and Boxing Day.
Tel: 01722 716338
Animal interactions. Alpaca herd and both indoor and outdoor play areas.

Older children may find something of interest at the **Cotswold Water Park** or be fascinated by the engines at **STEAM**. The latter may be equally interested in the **Swindon and Cricklade Railway**.

There are several paragliding schools in the county, particularly to the east where the downland edge offers take-off points. There are numerous possibilities for horse riding, the high downs being marvellous riding country. There is a go-kart track at Castle Combe's racing circuit. Swindon has a tenpin bowling alley and the **Oasis Leisure Centre** has a wave-making machine and flumes. Swindon also has a superb climbing wall at **The Link Centre**. For speed enthusiasts the **Castle Combe** race circuit and **Swindon Speedway** have annual programmes of races and events. For more leisurely fun, boat trips are available on the county's canals.

Sports

There are several large leisure centres in the county as well as other sports facilities. Not surprisingly, given the downland and the rural nature of the county, there are a number of high-quality golf courses. Information on all these is available at the Tourist Information Centres.

Cycling

The highest point in the county is at 965 feet (294m) on the Tan Hill–Milk Hill ridge in the Pewsey Vale at northern edge of the Salisbury Plain. Some downland approach roads are steep, but the climb is always short. Add the rural nature of the county and it can be seen that Wiltshire is ideal for the cyclist. A whole series of leaflets on worthwhile cycle routes (and on cycling on the downs in general) have been produced by Wiltshire Tourism and these are available at Tourist Information offices.

Walking

The Ridgeway is now part of an official National Trail, a long-distance path which links Avebury to the Thames valley, and has then been continued through the Chilterns to Ivinghoe Beacon. Technically the Ridgeway is a road and can be driven along much of its length, no matter how unreasonable such a use might seem. It occasionally is driven too, by four-wheel drive vehicles and motorcycles, though a series of voluntary bans means that for most of the time it is left to walkers, horse-riders and mountain bikers. The best of the ancient features along the way are reached easily from well-sited car parks, but the sections of county between these features – the high down, the long views – are one of the Ridgeway's joys. Short walks from the features are therefore worthwhile. The use of two cars or public transport to allow walking of longer sections of the route (which is entirely linear, though circular walks can be created) is better. Best, of course, is to follow the path: the section from the start, near Avebury, to Streatley, passing the finest ancient sites, is 42 miles (67km) long. The National Trail is waymarked and maintained.

From Avebury a continuation of the high downland walking has been organized into the **Wessex Ridgeway**. Though not official, the route is well waymarked and maintained by volunteers. It follows the chalk downland south to the Dorset coast. In part the Wessex Ridgeway follows the **Imber Range Perimeter Path**, which follows a circular route around the edge of the military holdings on Salisbury Plain, making the most of the access land for views and conservation areas.

Old Wardour Castle

Nature Reserves

There are dozens of high-quality Nature Reserves in the county, many set up and maintained by the Wiltshire Wildlife Trust. Some of these have been mentioned in the text, but a series of leaflets is available with details of the others. The leaflets are available from Tourist Information Offices or from:

Wiltshire Wildlife Trust
Elm Tree Court
Long Street
Devizes
Wiltshire
SN10 1NJ
Tel: 01380 725670
www.wiltshire-web.co.uk/wildlife

Arts and Crafts

As might be expected, the rural county of Wiltshire has a large number of arts and crafts people and outlets for their work. These can be found in most of the towns and larger villages, these also offering regular exhibitions of work.

Transport

The county has excellent train and bus services. Train information is, sadly, no easier to obtain in Wiltshire than anywhere else, but the position is much better for the buses. A leaflet – *Wiltshire County Transport Map and Guide* – is absolutely excellent, and is backed up by a telephone service – Wiltshire Travel Line on Tel: 08457 090899.

Tourist Information Centres

Amesbury
The Library
Smithfield Street
Amesbury SP4 7AL
Tel: 01980 622833

Bradford-on-Avon
50 St Margaret's Street
Bradford-on-Avon BA15 1DE
Tel: 01225 865797

Calne
Bank House
The Strand
Calne SN1 0EN
Tel: 01249 814000

Chippenham
The Citadel
Bath Road
Chippenham SN15 2AA
Tel: 01249 706333

Corsham
Arnold House
High Street
Corsham SN13 0EZ
Tel: 01249 714660

Cricklade
Town Council Office
The Old Weighbridge
116 High Street

Cricklade SN6 6AE
Tel: 01793 751394

Devizes
Cromwell House
Market Place
Devizes SN10 1JG
Tel: 01380 734669

Malmesbury
Town Hall
Market Lane
Malmesbury SN16 9BZ
Tel: 01666 823748

Marlborough
The Library
High Street
Marlborough SN8 1HD
Tel: 01672 513989

Melksham
Church Street
Melksham SN12 6LS
Tel: 01225 707424

Salisbury
Fish Row
Salisbury SP1 1EJ
Tel: 01722 334956

Swindon
37 Regent Street
Swindon SN1 1JL
Tel: 01793 530328

Trowbridge
St Stephen's Place
Trowbridge BA14 8AH
Tel: 01225 777054

Warminster
Central Car Park
Off Station Road
Warminster BA12 9BT
Tel: 01985 218548

Westbury
The Library
Edward Street
Westbury BA13 3BD
Tel: 01373 827158

Wootton Bassett
The Library
Borough Fields
Wootton Bassett
SN4 7DZ
Tel: 01793 850222

Other Useful Addresses

The National Trust
Wessex Regional Office
Eastleigh Court
Bishopstrow
Warminster BA12 9HW
Tel: 01985 843600

Visit Wiltshire Tourism Partnership
Economy Regeneration and Intelligence
Wiltshire County Council
County Hall
Bythesea Road

Trowbridge
Wiltshire BA14 8JN
Tel: 01225 713000
www.visitwiltshire.co.uk
The *Visit Wiltshire* website has general information for the visitor, and also has lists and brochures for accommodation from campsites through to luxury hotels.

Index

Published by
Landmark Publishing Ltd,
Ashbourne Hall, Cokayne Ave, Ashbourne, Derbyshire DE6 1EJ England
Tel: (01335) 347349 Fax: (01335) 347303 e-mail: landmark@clara.net
Website www.landmarkpublishing.co.uk

ISBN 13: 978 184306 387 2

British Library Cataloguing in Publication Data: a catalogue record for this
book is available from the British Library.

Print: Gutenberg Press, Malta
Design: Sarah Labuhn
Cartography: Sarah Labuhn

Front cover: Stonehenge at sunset
Back cover top: Westbury White Horse
Back cover bottom: Castle Combe village

Picture Credits

Jarrold Publishing: p59

All images below are supplied by Shutterstock, with credit to:
Matthew Collingwood: p3, 6, 11t, 82, back cover top; **Lance Bellers**: p11b
David Woolfenden: p26t, back cover bottom; **jon le-bon**: 47r; **Jack Larmour**: 38b
TTphoto: 38t; **Maria Townsend**: p62; **Stephen Inglis**: 78, front cover;
Susannah Grant: 102-103

All other photographs were supplied by Richard Sale